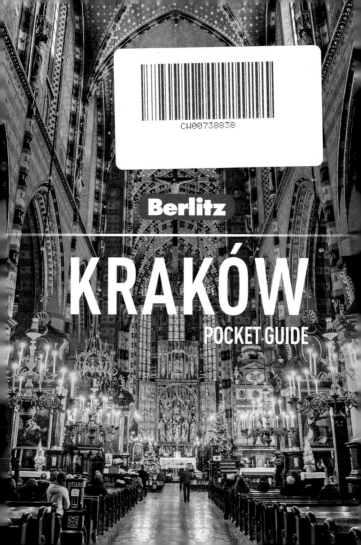

Berlitz

KRAKÓW

POCKET GUIDE

Walking Eye
mobile app

Discover the world's best destinations with the Insight Guides Walking Eye app, available to download for free in the App Store and Google Play.

The container app provides easy access to fantastic free content on events and activities taking place in your current location or chosen destination, with the possibility of booking, as well as the regularly-updated Insight Guides travel blog: Inspire Me. In addition, you can purchase curated, premium destination guides through the app, which feature local highlights, hotel, bar, restaurant and shopping listings, an A to Z of practical information and more. Or purchase and download Insight Guides eBooks straight to your device.

TOP 10 ATTRACTIONS

RYNEK GŁÓWNY
The medieval market square is Kraków's lively heart. See page 27.

NATIONAL MUSEUM
Where the best in Polish fine art, decorative arts and arms and armour can be seen. See page 69.

WAWEL
Ruling from its castle and cathedral, kings made this the centre of power in Poland for centuries. See page 44.

THE PLANTY
A restful ring of parkland surrounding the busy Old Town. See page 35.

ST MARY'S BASILICA
This medieval church is impressive inside and out. See page 28.

KAZIMIERZ
This cutting-edge district also offers a wealth of Jewish heritage. See page 50.

MUSEUM OF CONTEMPORARY ART (MOCAK)
See the best of Polish and international contemporary art in this stylish modern cultural centre. See page 60.

LORD'S ARK CHURCH
In the Communist showcase of Nowa Huta, this remarkable edifice stands apart as a monument to the Poles' fervent Catholic faith. See page 64.

AUSCHWITZ
Confront the face of evil at its two death camps. See page 72.

TARNÓW
A perfectly preserved Galician gem. See page 75.

A PERFECT DAY

9.00am

Breakfast

Start the day with breakfast at one of the numerous cafés (see page 101) in Rynek Główny. Look out for the carved animals – lizards, eagles, rams, even a rhinoceros – that give the merchant houses their names. The hourly Hejnał bugle call from the highest tower of St Mary's Basilica is your signal to get up and go.

11.00am

Back to college

At Kościół św. Anny, cut back into the city streets. At 11am in the courtyard of Collegium Maius, the ancient clock chimes the university tune (also 9am, 1pm, 3pm and 5pm).

11.30am

St Mary's Basilica

Back across the Rynek, peek inside the cathedral, to see the magnificent 15th-century altar carved by the 'Master of Nuremberg' Wit Stwosz.

Noon

Cloth Hall

Enjoy retail relief at the Sukiennice, otherwise known as the Cloth Hall, Kraków's main trading place since medieval times. Today it is as good a place as any to find amber jewellery, leather goods and traditional embroidery.

10.00am

Royal Route

Walk north up ul. Floriańska to the gate through which the kings of Poland entered the city to be crowned at Wawel. Leave behind the medieval Barbican and ul. św. Jana, to wander south through the leafy Planty.

2.00pm

Apostle alley

Crossing the Rynek past the tiny, ancient St Adalbert's church, rejoin the Royal Route on ul. Grodzka. At the line of apostles flanking the church of SS Peter and Paul, detour into ul. Kanonicza, Kraków's oldest and most beautifully preserved street.

3.00pm

Wawel's glory

It would take all day to see all the treasures on show at the castle and cathedral, but don't forget to climb the cathedral tower to touch the clapper of the huge 16th-century Zygmunt Bell – your wish will come true, so the story goes. Say goodbye to Wawel at the fire-breathing dragon statue which guards his cave on the riverbank.

1.00pm

Lunch

The streets to the west of Rynek Głowny are crammed with a fantastic array of eateries to suit all pockets. Locals throng to Chimera Salad Bar (see page 107), located in a cheerful cellar off ul. św. Anny.

10.30pm

Cool nightlife

If the food and music has revived you, make for Plac Nowy, centre of Kazimierz nightlife, begin barhopping with a drink at Alchemia on the corner of ul. Estery, and continue for as long as your energy and wallet allow.

7.00pm

Wild violins

Stroll down to ul. Szeroka, once the centre of Jewish Kazimierz. Book a table at Klezmer Hois (see page 111) or one of the other traditional restaurants around the square for an evening of Jewish food and lively klezmer music.

CONTENTS

INTRODUCTION

Kraków is considerably more than just cabbages and kings. Poland's magnificent cultural capital and ancient seat of royalty has been mesmerising visitors since the founding of the bishopric of Kraków on Wawel Hill in AD 1000. Located in the deep south of Poland, an hour or so north of the spectacular Tatra Mountains and just 100km (62 miles) from the Slovakian border, Kraków has a perfectly preserved Unesco-listed Old Town, an extraordinary Jewish heritage, bars and clubs in abundance and arguably the best selection of museums and galleries in the country. With attractions like these, it's not hard to see why the city plays host to almost 10 million visitors a year.

KrakowCard

While visiting Kraków is hardly expensive, the KrakowCard (www.krakowcard.com) is still a good deal. Valid for two days (100zł) or three (120zł), it gives free access to museums as well as unlimited travel on public transport. It's available online at www.krakowcard.com and can be collected at the DiscoverCracow tourist information points at ul. Św. Jana 2, ul. Rynek Glowny 30, ul. Św. Józefa 7, pl. Szczepański 8 and at the airport.

OLD TOWN TREASURES

Poland's second city, with just over 760,000 inhabitants, Kraków is one of the main urban areas in the Małopolska (Little Poland) region. At its centre is the only old town in a major Polish city to have escaped complete destruction during World War II. The Old Town's vast market square (Rynek Główny) has a dazzling array of glorious buildings. The Renaissance-style Cloth

Hall takes pride of place at the centre. The surrounding ensemble of buildings includes the twin-towered St Mary's Basilica, built during the 14th–16th centuries.

Leading away from the market square is a beguiling latticework of narrow streets. There are excellent museums and art galleries here; among them, the National Museum, a gallery of fine art with a collection that includes a

Facades on Kanonicza Street

rare painting by Leonardo da Vinci, *Lady with an Ermine*. With deep Catholic traditions, Kraków is the city whose archbishop went on to become Pope John Paul II. The house in which he lived as a young bishop is now the city's Archdiocesan Museum, located along ul. Kanonicza, the Old Town's only street to have been perfectly preserved as it was hundreds of years ago. Encircling the historic centre is the Planty, a delightful wooded park that marks the former location of the medieval city walls.

The Old Town is by no means the only reason to visit Kraków. Wawel, where the country's kings and queens were once crowned and now lie in state in the crypt of the cathedral, is a captivating primer in Polish history. The complex of buildings also includes medieval defensive walls and towers, the royal castle, treasury and armoury.

The nearby district of Kazimierz throws the horrors of World War II into sharp relief. A Jewish community that had thrived for

Portrait of Stanisław Wyspiański

over 450 years was obliterated during the German occupation of Kraków. Kazimierz is now making a comeback as a focal point of Jewish culture and heritage; it's also the city's number-one spot for hedonistic nightlife. Sights such as Kazimierz's Old Synagogue, the oldest surviving synagogue in Poland, and the moving exhibitions inside the Galicia Jewish Museum, rub shoulders with myriad bars and cafés packed nightly with the city's good-looking young crowd.

CULTURAL CAPITAL

Formerly the capital of Poland, and home to the country's oldest university (the Jagiellonian), Kraków also lays claim to be Poland's cultural capital. This largely conservative, academic and religious culture has, paradoxically, also nurtured revolutionary artists, such as the city's undisputed genius and leading member of the late 19th-century Young Poland (Młoda Polska) movement, Stanisław Wyspiański. The artist's sideways take on Polish life paved the way for a new generation of social commentators, who in their turn founded a number of galleries. Wyspiański's work, especially his wonderful stained-glass designs, can be found throughout the city. For contemporary art, including the occasional work of genius, the Palace of Art in the Old Town provides a fine temporary space for the city's up-and-coming artists. Many smaller independent galleries can be found around both the Old Town and in Kazimierz.

WAYS TO UNWIND

When the smoke and noise and chaos of the city get too much, Kraków provides plenty of good choices to slow down and unwind. Summer in Kraków can be a surprisingly hot and sticky affair at times, and city-dwellers seek relief in one of the 40 or so public parks, or, if they're lucky or rich enough, in the surrounding countryside where many like to keep a small summer cottage. Only the brave or foolish take to the city's waters, the River Wisła being little more than a squiggle of pollution that cuts Kraków in two. Located some 500km (300 miles) from the sea, Kraków has few bathing options, apart from the lakes around the city or the massive indoor Water Park (Park Wodny).

⊙ KRAKÓW'S FLOWER WOMEN

The tradition of selling flowers between the Cloth Hall and St Mary's Basilica on Kraków's main market square is believed to have started back in the first half of the 16th century. It is the sole preserve of women known as Krakowskie Kwiaciarki, or the Kraków Flower Women (*kwiat* means 'flower'). There are about 10 women selling flowers on the square in a business handed down almost exclusively from mother to daughter. The Kraków Flower Women are highly esteemed in the city, and have traditionally given flowers to visiting VIPs, including Popes Benedict XVI, John Paul II, Japanese Emperor Hirohito and Prince Charles. It's also their responsibility to lay flowers at the feet of the statue of the Polish author Adam Mickiewicz and hand out mistletoe to passers-by on Christmas Eve.

The city's Botanical Garden, the oldest in Poland, provide an opportunity to absorb nature in peaceful surroundings. As well as its tree-lined paths, immaculate gardens, ponds and hothouses, the Botanical Garden stages concerts during the summer. And for one night only in May, it opens its gates after dark as part of the city's delightfully different Museum Night (see page 95).

BEYOND THE TOWN CENTRE

Built just after World War II as a Communist showcase, the industrial district of Nowa Huta draws increasing numbers of visitors to see its monumental socialist-realist architecture.

A short distance southeast of Kraków are the Wieliczka salt mines. In an amazing feat of human labour and creativity, miners have carved solid salt into beautifully ornamented chapels – hundreds of metres below the ground.

There are also options for visitors with time for an extended excursion or two. To the south is Poland's winter capital, Zakopane. During the winter, the small town overflows with skiers from all over the country. Located at the foot of the Tatra Mountains, Zakopane is also very popular in summer, attracting thousands of visitors who use the town as a base for hiking trips in the pristine mountains and forests surrounding it.

An hour to the east of Kraków is Tarnów, one of the best-preserved medieval towns in Poland and a centre of Gypsy culture.

Finally, no trip to Kraków is complete without seeing the former Nazi death camps at Auschwitz, about 50km (30 miles) west of the city; a thought-provoking, uncomfortable and often deeply disturbing experience.

It's this mixture of the tragic and light-hearted, the old and the new, the conservative and the radical that makes Kraków such an extraordinary place to visit. Whatever your reason for visiting, your stay in Kraków will provide unique and unforgettable experiences.

A BRIEF HISTORY

The long and complex story of Kraków holds plenty of drama. Over the centuries, Poland's second city and former capital has been invaded, plundered, occupied and destroyed. Each time, the city proved resilient. In times of peace, Kraków has nurtured some of the finest scientific, religious and creative minds in Europe.

SETTLERS AND INVADERS

Evidence suggests that what is now Wawel Hill was inhabited by humans 50,000 years ago. Legend has it that a Slavic duke named Krak founded a fortified settlement on Wawel Hill, which was well positioned on key trade routes. The earliest recorded reference is dated AD 965, when Ibrahim ibn Jakub, a merchant from Cordoba in Spain, wrote that 'Krakwa' was a major town known throughout Europe.

In those days amber was a principal commodity in Kraków. It had been traded since the Neolithic era and was prized in the ancient world for its supposed medicinal benefits. It was also believed to bring the wearer good luck and both youthfulness and longevity. Salt from the

Amber for sale

Monument to the Battle of Grunwald

nearby Wieliczka salt mine was another valuable asset traded from Kraków.

Following Poland's conversion to Christianity in 966, the diocese of Kraków was founded in 1000, with the first cathedral built on Wawel Hill in the early 11th century. Wawel Hill became the royal residence in 1038, when King Kazimierz Odnowiciel (Casimir the Restorer), the patriarch of the Piast dynasty, moved the Polish capital from Gniezno to Kraków. The Tartar invasion of 1241 dealt a blow to this fledgling capital, but it was rapidly rebuilt. The municipal rights it was granted in 1257 established the layout of the centre (which remains the same today), including the Rynek (main market square), the first buildings of the Cloth Hall (Sukiennice), a covered market and the first city walls.

THE GOLDEN AGE

Under King Kazimierz Wielki (Casimir the Great, 1333–70), the last Piast monarch, Kraków and the country prospered. It is said that Kazimierz found Poland built of wood and left it built of stone. Important buildings erected during his reign include Wawel Castle, which was rebuilt and extended in Gothic style with walls, towers and links to the town's fortifications. Wawel Castle housed the first educational academy, established by the king in 1364, which later became the basis of the city's university. In 1335 he founded the town of Kazimierz, which became part of Kraków at the end of the 18th century.

In 1386 Władysław Jagiełło, the Grand Duke of Lithuania, was crowned king of Poland after he married the Polish queen, 11-year-old Jadwiga. Thus began the Jagiellonian dynasty (which lasted until 1572) and Poland's union (Commonwealth) with neighbouring Lithuania. On 15 July 1410, the Polish-Lithuanian army defeated the Teutonic Knights at the Battle of Grunwald. The victory was the military and political high point of the Commonwealth.

Kraków thrived under the Jagiellonians. As Europe's trade routes became ever busier, Kraków – strategically placed at the junction between Western Europe and Byzantium, and between Southern Europe and the Baltic and Scandinavia – grew in stature as a capital city and commercial centre.

Its significance was consolidated after it joined the Hanseatic League in 1430. Originally a commercial union of German towns on the Baltic coast, the league went on to promote maritime trade between countries around the Baltic and North seas. By the mid-15th century more than 150 towns were involved, and Kraków took advantage of lucrative trading opportunities. The resulting prosperity prompted German craftsmen and merchants, including Veit Stoss (Wit Stwosz), the master carver of Nuremberg, to visit or move to the town.

Phantom pigeons

The next time you shoo away one of the annoying pigeons in the Rynek, re-member this: for reasons that have been lost to time, legend has it that they are none other than the ghosts of the knights and courti-ers of Duke Henry (Henryk) IV Probus, senior prince of Poland from 1288 until his death in 1290.

The 16th century saw the development of trades and handicrafts, and the formation of more than 30 guilds. Towards the end of the 15th century, Kraków's printing presses produced the first books printed in Poland; the country's first postal service was established here a few decades later. Following the marriage of King Zygmunt Stary and the Italian princess Bona Sforza in 1518, there was an influx of renowned Italian architects. The legacy of Bartolomeo Berrecci, Giovanni Maria Padua and Santi Gucci can be seen at the Cloth Hall, Wawel Castle, and at various monuments, tombs and epitaphs.

Indeed, Kraków enjoys a distinct Italian Renaissance character. Its medieval defences were also extended at this time. The north of the town was protected by a Barbican and linked by

⊙ SARMATISM

Sarmatism was the predominant lifestyle and culture of the Polish *szlachta,* or nobility, from the 16th to the 19th century. It was based on the almost certainly fictitious belief that the Poles are the descendants of the Sarmatians, a group of people who lived north of the Black Sea from the 6th century BC to around the 3rd century AD. Polish Sarmatian culture evolved during the Renaissance from a movement of honourable pacifists into a full-blown warrior culture, which valued horse-riding skills and lavish oriental clothing (not to mention vast handlebar moustaches). Sarmatism faded away from the middle of the 18th century, but a pale shadow of it lives on in modern-day Kraków in the form of the Fowler Brotherhood (see page 66). The country's best collection of Sarmatian portraits can be viewed in Tarnów's District Museum (see page 75).

a double-walled thorough-fare to Floriańska Gate, one of eight city gateways.

AN ELECTED MONARCH

The Jagiellonian dynasty came to an end in 1572 with the death of King Sigismund II Augustus. The coronation of King Henryk Walezy (Henri de Valois) in 1574 was a minor landmark: he became the first Polish monarch to be elected – albeit by the nobility only – thus marking the end of

Wawel Castle

the country's hereditary system of government. Meanwhile, in the north, Warsaw was also rapidly developing as the capital of the Mazovian dukedom. More central to the Polish-Lithuanian Commonwealth than Kraków, Warsaw was becoming a leading administrative centre. The Sejm (parliament) was transferred to Warsaw in 1569, and Kraków went into decline. In 1596 King Zygmunt III Waza declared Warsaw the Polish capital and trans-ferred the royal residence to Warsaw's Royal Castle. The royal treasury remained at the Wawel, and coronations and royal funer-als continued to be held in Wawel Cathedral. King August II was the last king to be crowned here, in 1734.

In 1655-7 Kraków was badly damaged during the invasion by Sweden, one of the Polish-Lithuanian Commonwealth's most powerful rivals. Known locally as Potop ('The Deluge'), the invasion resulted in the looting of the royal treasury and many works of art.

*Wyspiański's 'God the Father',
in the Basilica of St Francis*

POLAND'S DECLINE

The opposition of various nobles to Poland's last king, Stanisław August Poniatowski, elected in 1764, heightened the country's vulnerability to its predatory neighbours. Prussia, Russia and Austro-Hungary partitioned Poland twice, in 1772 and 1793, and the country ceased to exist. Poles united and fought for independence. Tadeusz Kościuszko took a celebrated oath in Kraków's Rynek before leading his troops to victory over Russia at the Battle of Racławice in 1794. But a third partition, in 1795, forced the king to abdicate. The Kraków region became part of the Austro-Hungarian Empire. Kazimierz was incorporated into Kraków in 1791.

In 1809 the city became part of the Duchy of Warsaw, established by Napoleon. But in 1815 Napoleon was defeated at Waterloo and the subsequent Congress of Vienna designated Warsaw as the capital of a Russian-ruled Polish 'kingdom'. Kraków was given the status of a free city and capital of the Kraków Republic, which existed until 1846.

The Kraków revolution of that year was suppressed by the Austrians, who incorporated the city into their province of Galicia. Under the relatively liberal rule of the Austrians, Polish culture thrived. Then in 1850 the Great Fire of Kraków destroyed or seriously damaged almost 200 buildings, and once again the city had to rebuild. By the turn of the 20th century, Kraków had resumed its role as the country's intellectual and spiritual centre.

REBIRTH AND DISASTER

In 1914 at the beginning of World War I, a Polish army mobilised in Kraków. Led by Marshal Józef Piłsudski, by the end of the war it had defeated the Prussian, Russian and

---

⊙ STANISŁAW WYSPIAŃSKI

Born in Kraków on 15 January 1869, the architect, painter, playwright, poet and occasional cabinet-maker Stanisław Wyspiański's impact on the city is eclipsed only by God's late representative on Earth and Kraków's most famous son, Pope John Paul II. At the cutting edge of art during his brief lifetime, Wyspiański successfully blended traditional and modern styles to create a new and often controversial way of looking at both Poland under partition and the world in general. He's best remembered for his extraordinary stained-glass designs, several of which can be seen in Kraków. Wyspiański is also famous for writing what's considered by many to be Poland's most important play, *Wesele* (The Wedding), which was turned into a film by the Polish director Andrzej Wajda in 1973 and more recently by Wojciech Smarzowski. He was a leading member of Young Poland *(Młoda Polska)* art movement (1890–1918), a patriotic collective of artists, writers and musicians whose members included among others Xawery Dunikowski (see page 39) and Stanisław Ignacy Witkiewicz, aka Witkacy (see page 81). Plagued by physical and mental illness, Wyspiański died at the age of 38 on 28 November 1907. His body lies in Kraków's Pauline Church (see page 56).

Barbed wire encases the horrors of Auschwitz

Austro-Hungarian forces. Poland had finally won independence. Piłsudski acted as head of state until 1922; his state funeral was held in Kraków in 1935.

The Nazis invaded Poland on 1 September 1939, occupying Kraków less than a week later. They set up a puppet government, and the governor general, Hans Frank, took up residence in Wawel Castle. The Płaszów and Liban forced-labour camps were soon constructed, and a number of Jagiellonian University academics were sent to Sachsenhausen concentration camp. A Jewish ghetto was established in Kraków, from which Jews were sent to Auschwitz. There, more than 1 million prisoners, the great majority of them Jews from across Europe, together with Poles, Russians and Roma, died as a result of slavery, hunger, illness, torture or in the gas chambers. Corpses were burned in crematoria and buried in mass graves.

Before retreating in 1944, the Nazis began destroying evidence of their horrific crimes. They detonated the crematoria and some camp buildings, but didn't have enough time to destroy the gas chambers. The Nazis intended to raze Kraków but were foiled by a sudden advance by the Soviet Red Army. Kraków was thus one of the very few Polish cities to survive the war virtually intact. The Red Army liberated the city in January 1945.

THE POSTWAR YEARS

The Nazis left Warsaw devastated, so for a short time Kraków was once again the country's premier city. Rigged elections resulted in a Communist government, and the country became a satellite of the Soviet Union. The new regime was determined to replace the city's intellectual and cultural elitism with a new socialist spirit in the form of a vast proletarian labour force. The Lenin Steelworks, now known as Sendzimir, were built in the Kraków suburb of Nowa Huta in 1949–1956.

A key opponent of the repressive regime was the Catholic Church, which retained a level of independence during the Cold War years. The investiture of the archbishop of Kraków, Karol Wojtyła, as Pope John Paul II in 1978, and his visit to Poland in 1979, boosted opposition elements.

Lech Wałęsa's Solidarity movement mounted the most serious threat to an Eastern bloc regime since the Prague Spring of 1968. Bowing to the sheer weight of its numbers and

Polish Pope

It's hard to overstate the importance of the Catholic Church in Poland, a fact made clear in 1978 when Karol Wojtyła, the Polish cardinal and archbishop of Kraków, was elected to the papacy. Pope John Paul II was the first non-Italian to get the top job for over 400 years.

international support, the government accepted it as a legal trade union in 1980. But the following year, Prime Minister General Jaruzelski introduced martial law and banned Solidarity. This was a time of severe shortages – people had to queue all night for staples – and meat, butter and even vodka were rationed. Artificial employment provided work, however menial or unnecessary, for everyone. Martial law was lifted in 1983, triggered by the second visit to his homeland of John Paul II.

Waves of strikes in the spring and autumn of 1988 led to talks between the Communist Party and the leaders of Solidarity. A path towards democracy was mapped out. The Communists were soundly beaten in the election of June 1989, and the Polish Communist Party was dissolved in January 1990. Privatisation of state-run companies began in 1994.

The newly independent country began to look outwards. Poland joined Nato in 1999 and the European Union in 2004. Kraków served as European City of Culture in 2000.

TODAY'S KRAKÓW

The economic reforms and rise in living standards that Poland has experienced since 1989 have been particularly noticeable in Kraków. Café society has returned, restaurants have boomed, shops stock top international brand names and premium-quality Polish products, and standards of service have improved. Pollution from the Nowa Huta steelworks – detrimental to people and historic buildings alike – has been much reduced. Unfortunately, smog generated by coal-fired furnaces still haunts the city during winter. The annual Jewish Festival of Culture, which which begun in 1988 as a small academic gathering, has blossomed into a major event, reviving the city's Jewish heritage. Above all, Kraków is now firmly on the international tourist map – with millions visiting every year.

HISTORICAL LANDMARKS

50,000 BC People are living in the Wawel Hill area.

9000–4500 BC Tribes of hunter-gatherers appear in the Kraków area.

AD 965 Cordoba merchant Ibrahim ibn Jakub refers to 'Krakwa'.

990–999 Kraków is incorporated into Poland by Mieszko I or Bolesław I the Brave who builds Wawel and the city's first cathedral.

1000 The diocese of Kraków is founded.

1038 Casimir the Restorer moves his capital to Kraków from Gniezno.

1241 Tartars destroy Kraków.

1290 Construction of St Mary's Basilica begins.

1333 Casimir the Great, the last of the Piast dynasty, is crowned king.

1335 Casimir the Great founds Kazimierz.

1364 Kraków Academy (today's Jagiellonian University) is founded.

1385 Lithuanian Grand Duke Władysław Jagiełło is crowned king.

1495 Kraków's Jews are forced to move into neighbouring Kazimierz.

1596 The nation's capital is moved from Kraków to Warsaw.

1772 First partition of Poland.

1794 Kosciuszko Uprising begins.

1795 Third partition of Poland; Kraków joins Austro-Hungarian Empire.

1918 Poland regains independence; Kraków is the first major free city.

1939–44 The Nazis murder most of Kraków's large Jewish population.

1945 Imposition of Communist rule.

1978 Karol Wojtyła becomes Pope John Paul II.

1981 Imposition of martial law by General Jaruzelski.

1989 Talks between the government and Solidarity lead to elections.

2002 Jacek Majchrowski is elected Mayor of Kraków.

2004 Poland joins the European Union.

2010 The body of the Polish President Lech Kaczynski is interred at Wawel.

2015 Andrzej Duda, a lawyer from Kraków, is elected President of Poland.

2016 Kraków hosts World Youth Day, a gathering of around 3 million young people, which is also attended by Pope Francis.

2018 Municipal elections are held in Kraków, with Majchrowski running for a fifth term as mayor.

The grand Wawel Cathedral

WHERE TO GO

Most visitors to Kraków are drawn to its Old Town, one of the most beautiful in Europe and the only important historical town in Poland to escape destruction in World War II. The two other main sights, Wawel and Kazimierz, are immediately south of the Old Town, making exploration of Kraków very easy. Off the well-trodden tourist path lie any number of treasures, ranging from some of the city's best museums to the emerging Holocaust trail in Podgórze, south of the Wisła (Vistula) River. The northeastern district of Nowa Huta provides a snapshot of Poland's Communist past, while to the west, near the town of Oświęcim, are the former Nazi death camps at Auschwitz. Southeast of the city in Wieliczka are the extraordinary, Unesco-listed salt mines. Further afield, towns such as Tarnów and the mountain resort of Zakopane offer those with time on their hands a chance to experience the region to the full.

THE OLD TOWN: RYNEK GŁÓWNY

Among Poland's impressive market squares, Kraków's immense 200m x 200m (656ft x 656ft) **Rynek Główny ❶** is the undisputed king. The focal point of Kraków's wonderful Old Town (Stare Miasto), and an ideal starting point for exploring the city, the Rynek was laid out in 1257, and at the time was the largest square in Europe. Long a thriving centre of commerce, the Rynek retains this commercial bustle, while also being the city's primary tourist magnet. It offers a host of things to see and do as well as providing a ring of outdoor cafés for sitting and watching the world go by during the summer months.

ST MARY'S BASILICA

Of the two main sights fighting for supremacy (the other being the magnificent Cloth Hall), the twin-towered **St Mary's Basilica** ❷ (Kościół Mariacki; www.mariacki.com; Mon–Sat 11.30am–6pm, Sun 2–6pm) in the square's northeastern corner has a slight edge over its commercial cousin. The Gothic exterior dates from the 14th century, although what really makes this church one of the city's highlights is found inside. The colour and intricacy of the triple-naved interior is breathtaking; it includes 19th-century murals by Jan Matejko, extraordinary stained glass by Stanisław Wyspiański and a massive late-Gothic altarpiece called *The Lives of Our Lady and Her Son Jesus Christ*, which was completed between 1477–89 by the German master carver Veit Stoss (Wit Stwosz).

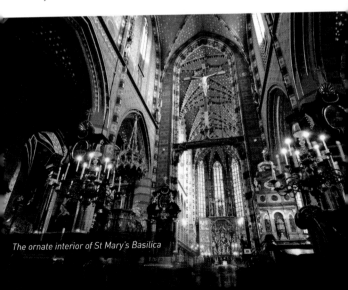

The ornate interior of St Mary's Basilica

The view from the northernmost **tower** (Apr–Oct Tue–Sat 9.10–11.30am and 1.10–5.30pm, Sun 1.10–5.30pm; Nov–Dec and Mar Thu–Sat 9.10–11.30am and 1.10–5.30pm) is worth the struggle up the 239 steps. Every day, on the hour, a trumpeter sounds his horn from here. The abrupt pause recalls a legendary watchman who, on sighting Tartar invaders, raised the alarm and was silenced by an arrow.

Next to St Mary's on Plac Mariacki is **St Barbara's Church** (Kościół św. Barbary). Dating from the 14th century, this was the main Polish site of worship in the city under Austrian occupation, when German was still the main language in use in the basilica next door. Just outside the entrance on the left is a 16th-century sculpture of *Gethsemane*, while inside the main points of interest are the 15th-century stone *Pietà* and the superb 18th-century painted ceiling.

CLOTH HALL

At the centre of the Rynek is the imposing **Cloth Hall** ❸ (Sukiennice; Nov–Apr daily 9am–5pm, May–Oct daily 9am–7pm), which started life as a small shed for storing goods around the time the Rynek was laid out in the 13th century. The Cloth Hall's current appearance owes most to the Italian architect Giovanni il Mosca, who in the 16th century gave it its predominantly Renaissance look. Today's Cloth Hall is home to a ground-floor **market** selling folk crafts, jewellery, leather goods and souvenirs, and the long-running **Noworolski Café** (see page 101). Upstairs is the oldest branch of the National Museum in Kraków, featuring a **gallery** of 19th-century Polish paintings (Tue–Sat 10am–6pm, Sun until 4pm). It was Poland's first national museum and includes work by Poland's greatest painters, such as Jan Matejko. On the ground floor of the Sukiennice, near the Kraków information office, you will find the entrance

Browsing the stalls in the Cloth Hall

to a branch of the city's historical museum – **Rynek Underground** (Podziemia Rynku; www.podziemia rynku.com; Nov–Mar Wed–Mon 10am–8pm, Tue 10am–4pm, Apr–Oct Wed–Sun 10am–10pm, Mon until 8pm and Tue until 4pm; closed second Tue in the month; free every Tue; online booking essential). This archaeological exhibition shows the historical development of the Rynek area and has several interactive displays that both children and adults will enjoy.

TOWN HALL TOWER

On the other side of the building is another branch of the Historical Museum of the City of Kraków (www.mhk.pl), housed inside the **Town Hall Tower** ❹ (Wieża Ratuszowa; only Apr–Oct daily 10.30am–6pm; closed second Tue in the month). The tower is all that remains of the 14th-century Town Hall, ravaged by fire and pulled down by the Austrians in the early 19th century. The 68m (223ft) tower is now home to a small collection of old photographs, clothing and a historic timepiece now synchronised with the atomic clock in Mainflingen. A 110-step climb takes you to a **viewing platform** offering an excellent panorama.

Beside the tower is a striking-looking sculpture of a hollow head, lying on its side, that local children love to climb around inside. This is *Eros Bendato*, the work of the Polish sculptor

Igor Mitoraj (1944–2014), who studied at Kraków's Academy of Art. Originally a painter, Mitoraj's sculptures are all based on the human form and most feature bandages of some description, looking at the same time like fractured contemporary visions and broken statues of antiquity. Two smaller pieces can be seen in the National Museum (see page 69).

OTHER SIGHTS IN THE RYNEK

The diminutive **St Adalbert's Church** ❺ (Kościół św. Wojciecha; http://wojciechnarynku.pl) is to the southeast of the Cloth Hall. The earliest parts of the building date back to the 11th century, making it older than the Rynek and every other church in the city. It's a beguiling jumble of pre-Roman, Roman, Gothic, Renaissance and Baroque. Inside, just six rows of humble wooden pews are arranged on a floor that sits some 2m (6.5ft) below the surface of the surrounding market square. In the church vaults is a small **archaeological exhibition** (Mon and Wed–Sat 10am–4pm, Tue until 2pm; www.ma.krakow.pl).

Immediately east of the Cloth Hall is the **Adam Mickiewicz Monument** ❻ (Pomnik Adama Mickiewicza), one of the most famous statues in Poland. Strangely enough, the country's foremost 19th-century Romantic poet never visited Kraków and lived much of his life in exile. He is also

Midnight museums

For one night every May, many of Kraków's museums open until midnight or later, presenting their usual exhibits in an unusual way. Highlights include the amazing Night of the Hassidim in Kazimierz's Old Synagogue, and a wonderful chance to see the Botanical Garden in a new light. Tickets can be bought from any Kraków information office, though the queues for the popular ones may be long.

Inside a Gothic cupola in St Adalbert's Church

claimed by the Lithuanians (who call him Adomas Mickevičius) as one of their own. Mickiewicz's most famous work, the epic poem *Pan Tadeusz*, opens with the line 'Lithuania, my country!', adding to the confusion. The poet died in Constantinople in 1855. Some 35 years later his remains were brought to Kraków and laid to rest in the crypt of Wawel Cathedral, an event that inspired a competition to build the monument, which was won by Teodor Rygier. Rygier's work, unveiled in 1898 to celebrate the centenary of the poet's birth, was destroyed by the Germans during World War II. The current statue dates from 1955 and is a popular meeting place.

AROUND THE EDGES

The Rynek's scores of cafés are located in superb merchant houses, each of which has a story to tell. Now beautifully restored, most have a symbol over the door from which they take their names – look out for lizards, rams and eagles. In the far northwestern corner, the main branch of the **Historical Museum of the City of Kraków** ❼ (Tue–Sun 10am–5.30pm). Founded in 1899, the museum is housed inside Italian architect Baldassare Fontana's spectacular Pałac Krzysztofory (Palace Under St Christopher). Its wing houses temporary exhibitions and one permanent one – Cyberteka, which features multimedia displays and 3D films of the spatial and urban development of Kraków from pre-incorporation times to 1909–15.

Just off the Rynek, opposite St Mary's Basilica, is the highly recommended **Bourgeois House** ❽ (Nov–Mar Wed and Fri–Sun 9am–4pm, Thu noon–7pm; Apr–Oct Wed–Sun 10am–5.30pm; free on Wed; www.mhk.pl), also known as the **Hippolit House** (Kamienica Hipolitów) after a rich

⊘ LENIN IN KRAKÓW

On a bright midsummer morning on 22 June 1912, Vladimir Ilyich Lenin arrived in Kraków on the overnight train from Vienna. He wished to be closer to his beloved Russia, whose borders, at the time, ran just a few kilometres to the north. Living in a rented apartment with his wife and mother-in-law, the 42-year-old divided his time between planning a revolution, eating smoked salmon, listening to Beethoven, visiting Noworolski Café (see page 101) and, during the harsh Polish winters, ice skating near the city's Botanical Garden.

Lenin spent his two Galician summers in the village of Poronin near Zakopane, where he organised a conference of Bolshevik leaders. Agents infiltrated the conference and arranged for his arrest by the Austrian police as a Russian spy on 8 August 1914. Briefly imprisoned, Lenin was soon released and left for Switzerland, never to return.

Mały Rynek (Little Market Square)

16th-century merchant family who once lived in the building. Each room has been painstakingly set out with authentic furniture in a succession of periods from the 17th century until the first half of the 20th century. The entrance is found on the right inside the hallway of the building. Colourful façades adorn nearby **Little Market Square** 9 (Mały Rynek), once the site of meat, fish and poultry vendors.

THE OLD TOWN: AROUND THE RYNEK

What is now known as the Old Town was founded by Bolesław the Shy (1226–79) and built to replace a group of small settlements destroyed by the Tartar invasion of 1241. The Old Town received its municipal (Magdeburg Law) rights in 1257. It was populated by settlers primarily from the German-speaking region of Silesia, and was for its first few years a city ruled by

Germans. On 1 September 1306, an army led by Władysław the Short (1261–1333) invaded the city, leaving 2,000 dead Germans in its wake. Fifteen years later in 1320, he was crowned king of Poland in Wawel Cathedral, and thus began Kraków's so-called Golden Age.

Somewhat surprisingly, much of the city's wonderful grid-like Old Town remains relatively untouched by the creeping claws of tourism. Around the Rynek is a marvellous higgledy-piggledy collection of fine old buildings. They house everything from some of Poland's best museums to the occasional saucy nightclub. It is rewarding to take a lazy wander through the quiet backstreets, which are lined with historic town houses, fine churches and delightful small shops.

The Old Town's **Royal Route** (Trakt Królewski) is the traditional way that new Polish kings and queens arrived for their coronations. Splitting the Old Town in two from north to south, it starts at the Barbican (see page 36), runs down ul. Floriańska, through the Rynek and south along ul. Grodzka to Wawel (see page 44).

Encircling the whole of the Old Town is the **Planty** ❿, a ring of relaxing green space. The Planty marks the former location of massive fortifications and a wide moat that once protected the city from attack.

The Planty

Of the 40 or so parks in Kraków, the Planty, a wonderful 21-hectare (52-acre) ring of green around the Old Town, is the most obvious choice for an escape from the incessant racket of the city centre. Situated on the site of the city's former medieval defensive walls, knocked down in the early part of the 19th century, it is made up of some 30 individual gardens and is full of trees, sculptures and, in summer, several cafés.

AROUND THE BARBICAN AND UL. FLORIAŃSKA

At the far northern end of ul. Floriańska, through the 14th-century Brama Floriańska (Florian's Gate), is the **Barbican** ⓫ (Barbakan; www.mhk.pl; Apr–Oct daily 10.30am–6pm; closed every second Monday of the month), a branch of the city's historical museum. Built in 1498, this fort was once the city's northern defence point. With its seven turrets and walls 3m (10ft) thick, the Barbican is, along with Florian's Gate, the oldest surviving part of the city's medieval defences. Visitors can walk around the two ramparts, there's a small exhibition in the main courtyard and occasionally historical re-enactments in the summer. A short section of the 13th century City Defence Walls is also accessible (entry tickets cover both the Barbican and the Walls).

Just northeast of the Barbican, and not technically part of the Old Town, is the large **Grunwald Monument** (Pomnik Grunwaldzki) on pl. Matejki. The Battle of Grunwald (in German 'Tannenberg', in Lithuanian 'Žalgiris') took place between a combined Polish-Lithuanian army and the Teutonic Knights on 15 July 1410 and resulted in the defeat of the Knights. One of Poland's proudest moments, the battle was commemorated on its 500th anniversary in 1910 by the unveiling of this monument in front of an estimated 160,000 people. It features the Polish king Władysław Jagiełło riding his horse and flanked by representatives of the Polish and Lithuanian armies. In front of them, his cousin, the Lithuanian prince Vytautas (Witold), stands over the dead Urlich von Jungingen, the Teutonic Knights' Grand Master. The current statue is a copy from 1976, made from models and drawings of the original destroyed by the occupying Germans during World War II.

Back on ul. Floriańska and south past the Barbican on the left-hand side is the **Jan Matejko House** ⓬ (Dom Jana Matejki; http://mnk.pl; Tue–Sat 10am–6pm, until 4pm on Sun), a branch of the National Museum in Kraków. The artist Jan Matejko was

Florian's Gate

born here in 1838. A one-time teacher of Stanisław Wyspiański (see page 21), Matejko won a place in the hearts of the nation with his vast oil paintings depicting epic moments from Polish history. The museum tells the story of the artist's life in pictures, documents and personal possessions as well as multimedia installations. Not far from Matejko's house, beside the Barbican, is a monument of the artist sitting within a large picture-frame.

Further down ul. Floriańska is the quirky **Pharmacy Museum** (Muzeum Farmacji; http://muzeum.farmacja.uj.edu. pl/; Tue noon–6.30pm, Wed–Sat 9.30am–3pm), a beautifully restored, 15th-century burgher's house stuffed full of rec-reations of old apothecaries, jars of pickled snakes and other medicine-related odds and ends.

In the northeastern corner of the Old Town on pl. św. Ducha is the wedding-cake **Juliusz Słowacki Theatre** (Teatr im. Juliusza Słowackiego; www.slowacki.krakow.pl). Styled on the Paris Opera and controversially built on the site of a medieval church demolished to make way for it, it was opened in 1893 and hides a few lavish treats inside. It's not officially open for tours, but if you attend a theatre or opera performance here, you'll see the gilded

CZARTORYSKI MUSEUM

Just to the west of the Floriańska Gate on ul. św. Jana, some of the city's finest works of art belong to the **Czartoryski Museum** (Muzeum Czartoryskich), another branch of the National Museum in Kraków. The museum is closed for restoration until 2019. The museum's most popular treasures, Leonardo da Vinci's *Lady with an Ermine*, is displayed in the main building of the National Museum at ul. 3 Maja (see page). On the corner of ul. św. Jana and ul. św. Tomasza is the diminutive

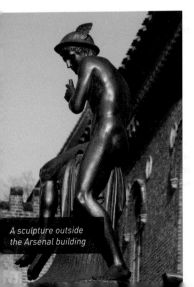

A sculpture outside the Arsenal building

Church of St John the Baptist and St John the Evangelist (Kościół św. Jana Chrzciciela i św. Jana Ewangelisty). The church predates the Old Town, which accounts for the kink in the road immediately south of the building (known to the locals as the Doubting Thomas Nook). However, the original 12th-century Romanesque building was extensively remodelled (to the point of being almost entirely rebuilt) during the first half of the 17th century, which explains the church's Baroque appearance. The interior is relatively plain, the main interest being the 16th-century altar painting, *The Mother of God Redeeming the Slaves*.

THE PALACE OF FINE ART AND THE FELIKS JASIEŃSKI SZOŁAYSKI HOUSE

Situated on pl. Szczepański (Szczepański square) in the northwest is the **Palace of Fine Art** (Pałac Sztuki; http://palac-sztuki.krakow.pl/; Mon–Fri 8.15am–6pm, Sat–Sun 10am–6pm). The early 20th-century neo-Baroque building hosts hit-and-miss exhibitions of contemporary art, and is the city's most active nurturer of new artists. In the entrance hall is a lovely wooden bust of Xawery Dunikowski (1875–1964) holding a tiny church in his hand. Dunikowski was an artist and sculptor who lived a long and fascinating life. An Auschwitz survivor, his death camp-inspired art and other work in general is worth looking out for.

Nearby is the **Feliks Jasieński Szołayski House** ⓭ (http://mnk.pl; Tue–Sat 10am–6pm, Sun 10am–4pm), a branch of the National Museum, housing permanent and temporary exhibitions as well as organising lectures, concerts and art lessons for children and young people. It used to house the Wyspiański Museum; the collection is currently under renovation, although part of it can be seen in the main building of the National Museum until January 2019, see 69. From pl. Szczepański it is well worth taking a short detour to see the ultra-modern façade of the Malopolska Garden of Arts (Małopolski Ogród Sztuki, ul. Rajska 12; www.mos.art.pl), a cultural centre for contemporary theatre, cinema, visual arts, dance and music.

JAGIELLONIAN UNIVERSITY

A short walk west of the Rynek is the **Jagiellonian University Museum** (Muzeum Uniwersytetu Jagiellońskiego; tel: 012 663

On a tour in the courtyard of the Collegium Maius

15 21/663 13 07; www.maius.uj.edu.pl; guided tours only: Sat 10am–1.30pm, Apr–Oct Mon, Mon, Wed, Fri 10am–2.20pm, Tue, Thu 10am–5.20pm, Nov–Mar Mon–Fri 10am–2.20pm; English language tours at 1pm, booking essential; cash only). It's housed in the **Collegium Maius** ⓮, Europe's third-oldest (and Poland's first) university college, founded in 1364. Nicolas Copernicus (Mikolaj Kopernik), who formulated our modern theory of the solar system, is believed to have begun studying here in 1492.

The museum, which contains artefacts from the university's collection, can only be seen on a guided tour. Starting under the great clock in the arcaded cloister, tours take in the best of the interiors – including ornate academic halls, the treasury, library and professors' dining hall – as well as objects such as oil paintings, ancient books and a range of old scientific instruments. One of the most precious possessions is the oldest globe depicting the Americas still in existence. Five times a day (9am, 11am, 1pm, 3pm, 5pm), the courtyard clock plays the university tune *Gaudeamus Igitur* and figures from Kraków's history parade across the clockface.

BASILICA OF ST FRANCIS AND DOMINICAN CHURCH

On either side of ul. Grodzka, at the intesection with pl. Wszystkich Świętych, are two particularly impressive churches. To the west, the **Basilica of St Francis of Assisi** ⑮ (Bazylika św. Franciszka z Asyżu; www.franciszkanska.pl; Mon–Sat 10am–4pm, Sun 1.15–4pm) was the first brick building in the city when it was constructed in 1269. Like so many other houses of worship in the city, the basilica has seen numerous structural and decorative changes over the centuries, including the addition of several Wyspiański stained-glass windows installed between 1895 and 1904 at the front and back of the building. This is perhaps the best place to see his work in all its glory. The large *Act of Creation* depicts God in wild streaks of colour; Wyspiański is believed to have based the face of God on that of a beggar. The walls and ceiling are covered in bright Art Nouveau designs, which are radical almost beyond belief, especially set against the austere Gothic wooden confessionals.

Head east from here to the imposing **Dominican Church** (Kościół Dominikanów), which is located on the site of the city's original marketplace. The church was completed in around 1250 and originally belonged to an order of monks from Bologna. The lavish interior was gutted by a fire in 1850 and remodelled in a far more sober manner in 1872. Of particular interest inside the immense building are the huge Gothic wooden altars and the image of *Our Lady of the Rosary* inside the Rosary Chapel, which is reputed to have special healing powers.

SOUTH ALONG UL. GRODZKA

You'll find a couple of diversions in the area immediately south-west of pl. Wszystkich Świętych and ul. Grodzka, courtesy of two of Kraków's less well-known museums. Of narrow appeal is the very small **Geology Museum** (Muzeum Geologiczne; www.ing.pan.pl; Thu–Fri 10am–3pm, Sat 10am–2pm; free last Sat of the month) on ul. Senacka 3. It consists of a handful of glass cases full of various rocks and crystals found in the area. The exhibits are labelled in Polish only.

Around the corner, on ul. Poselska, is the larger and far better **Archaeology Museum** (Muzeum Archeologiczne; www.ma.krakow.pl; Sept–June Mon, Wed, Fri 9am–3pm, Tue, Thu 9am–6pm, Sun 11am–4pm; July–Aug Mon–Fri 10am–5pm, Sun 10am–3pm). Exhibits include models showing how life looked

The Twelve Apostles atop Ss Peter and Paul's Church

in the Małopolska region of southern Poland over the past several thousand years, an outstanding collection of local clothing from 70,000 BC up until the construction of the Old Town, and a few rooms given over to ancient Egypt.

STS. PETER AND PAUL'S CHURCH

On the eastern side of ul. Grodzka is **Sts. Peter and Paul's Church ⑯** (Kościół św. Piotra i św. Pawła; Tue–Sat 9am–5pm, Sun 1.30–5.30pm; http://apostolowie.pl), an early 16th-century Baroque masterpiece. Kraków's main Jesuit church has changed hands numerous times over the centuries, but is now back with its rightful owners. The striking statues of the Twelve Apostles guarding the entrance are copies of the 18th-century originals. The crypt contains the remains of the priest, Piotr Skarga (1536–1612), whose controversial statue, looking more like a superhero, stands in the small square just across the street.

UL. KANONICZA

Originally part of a tiny hamlet called Okół that became a part of Kraków in 1410, **ul. Kanonicza ⑰**, which runs parallel to ul. Grodzka, is the one street in the Old Town that's been kept as it was, with no annoying signs, glitzy shops or burger bars. The street is sacred to the Poles as being the former home of a young and rather sporty Karol Wojtyła, who became Pope John Paul II in 1978 after serving as archbishop of Kraków.

Much of the street belongs to the Catholic Church, including Wojtyła's former seminary, now the city's **Archdiocesan Museum ⑱** (Muzeum Archidiecezjalne; www.muzeumkra. diecezja.pl; Tue–Fri 10am–4pm, Sat–Sun 10am–3pm) at no. 19. It's brimming with religious goodies from the 13th century to the present day.

WAWEL

Wawel ⓳ is Poland's grand symbol of patriotism, independence, pride and hope, an extraordinary ensemble of buildings perched on top of a 50m (165ft) rock at the southern tip of the Old Town. The complex offers an A–Z of Polish history and nobility within the pleasurable confines of its four fortified walls, containing a wealth of exhibits inside its mostly Romanesque and Gothic structures.

Evidence exists of human life on Wawel Hill 50,000 years ago. The first major structure on the site was the first cathedral, built in 1020. Construction work on the buildings you see today began when Kraków became the Polish capital in 1038, though many additions were made in subsequent centuries under different rulers. Wawel's most notable features date from the period 1507–36, when the Italians Francesco the Florentine and Bartolomeo Berrecci oversaw a major series of changes. In World War II, the Nazis made Wawel their headquarters, and the area narrowly escaped being turned to rubble when they retreated.

Wawel's popularity means that visiting, especially during the busy summer tourist season, has been limited to a certain number of tourists

Wawel Hill

each day, making booking in advance at Wawel Visitor Centre highly recommended (tel: 012 422 16 97; www.wawel.krakow.pl; the hill is open: Nov–Feb 6am–5pm, Mar, Oct until 6pm, Apr, Sep 7pm, May, Aug 8pm, and Jun, Jul, until 9pm, Sept–Mar closed on Mon). Wawel covers a large area, so be sure to pick up a free map at the information centre (see page 49). The full Wawel experience can

Sacred art

The beautifully restored building at Kanonicza 17 is the Ciołek Palace (Pałac Ciołka; Tue–Sat 10am–6pm, till 4pm on Sun) built between 1501–03 for the bishop of Płock, Erazm Ciołek. It houses a branch of the National Museum in Kraków including some priceless Orthodox icons and a gallery of Polish art dating from the 12th–18th centuries.

take at least a day if you want to see everything at a leisurely pace. If time is limited, be sure to visit at least the cathedral and, inside the castle, the Crown Treasury and Armoury.

THE CATHEDRAL

An unmissable sight is the **cathedral** ❷⓪ (Katedra Wawelska; www.katedra-wawelska.pl; Apr–Oct Mon–Sat 9am–5pm, Sun 12.30–5pm; Nov–Mar Mon–Sat 9am–4pm, Sun 12.30–4pm, Cathedral Museum closed Sun; Cathedral free, charge for Zygmunt Bell, Royal Tombs Cathedral Museum and four chapels). The cathedral was built here soon after the founding of the diocese of Kraków in 1000. The current cathedral, technically the third to stand on the site, dates primarily from the 14th century and is considered by many to be the most important building in the country. Although less impressive than St Mary's Basilica, Wawel Cathedral features a wealth of statues, chapels and tombs among its highlights. Dominating everything as you enter is the

Inside Wawel Cathedral

grand tomb of the former bishop of Kraków, St Stanisław (1030–79), who, according to legend, was murdered by Bolesław II the Bold, and to whom the cathedral is dedicated.

The cathedral contains a total of 18 chapels. Each one has its own intrinsic beauty, but the most spectacular is the 15th-century Holy Cross Chapel (on the right as you enter), complete with some extraordinary Russian murals painted in 1470. Also in this chapel is Kazimierz IV's 1492 marble sarcophagus, the work of Veit Stoss.

Entrance to the main building is free. You have to pay for a full visit, which takes in the **Royal Crypts** and a trip up the winding wooden stairs to view the 11-tonne **Zygmunt Bell**. The crypts are where 10 of Poland's former kings and their wives, as well as many other important figures, including the poet and patriot Adam Mickiewicz and Poland's military hero Józef Piłsudski, lie in their tombs. Controversially, in 2010, Poland's president Lech Kaczyński joined their number after dying in the Smolensk plane crash.

The massive bell was cast in 1520, and can be heard some 50km (31 miles) away.

The adjoining **Cathedral Museum** was opened in 1978 by Karol Wojtyła immediately prior to his accession to the papacy. A highly recommended diversion, it contains some of Poland's most precious religious and regal possessions, dating from the 13th century onwards. The Cathedral Museum is best enjoyed with a visit to the Archdiocesan Museum (see page 43) if you want to get the full flavour and significance of the long relationship between the city and the Church.

CASTLE HIGHLIGHTS

At the eastern edge of the Renaissance-style courtyard are the **State Rooms** (Reprezentacyjne Komnaty Królewskie) and **Royal Private Apartments** (Prywatne Apartamenty Królewskie; Apr–Oct Tue–Fri 9.30am–5pm, Sat–Sun 10am–5pm; Nov–Mar Mon–Sat 9.30am–4pm, only State Rooms Nov–Mar Sun 10am–4pm and free, admission to the Royal Private Apartments in groups of up to 10, guided tours only, charge includes guide service).

⊘ THE WAWEL-AKROPOLIS

Stanisław Wyspiański's connections with Kraków include an extensive attachment to Wawel dating back to childhood. Wawel features in many of his works, including poems, his first play, *Legend* (1898), and a number of unfulfilled designs for Wawel Cathedral. His masterpiece was a complete redesign of the castle complex, the 'Wawel-Akropolis', motivated by the Austrian army's plans to move their barracks out of Wawel and into new premises. Throughout the winter of 1904–5 Wyspiański, with the help of the architect Władysław Ekielski, worked on a project to remove the parts of Wawel built by the Austrian occupiers, and add a series of buildings, towers and even an amphitheatre. His intention was to create a vision of Poland as the mighty nation it once was. Illness prevented progress beyond a series of drawings, and the work was never completed.

On display in a seemingly never-ending series of breathtaking rooms are intricate carved furniture, some wonderful oil portraits and a series of huge and delightful 16th-century Flemish tapestries. Highlights of the State Rooms include the magnificent Bird Room, the Eagle Hall and the Senators' Hall. Keep an eye out for the extraordinary medieval wallpaper.

Located in the northeastern corner of the courtyard, to the left of the State Rooms, is another highly recommended sight, the **Crown Treasury and Armoury** (Skarbiec Koronny i Zbrojownia; Apr–Oct Mon 9.30am–1pm, Tue–Fri until 5pm, Sat–Sun 10am–5pm, Nov–Mar Tue–Sat 9.30am–4pm). The most renowned exhibit is *Szczerbiec* ('notched sword'), Poland's original (12th- or 13th-century) coronation sword. Among the other treasures are Poland's Crown Jewels, intricately etched golden platters and goblets, old coins and an intimidating, albeit dazzling, array of military equipment. There's a room full of huge spears, a

⊙ DRAGON'S DEN

Like all old cities, Kraków has a number of legends. One of them concerns a mythical dragon by the name of Smok Wawelski, who lived in a cave on Wawel and favoured a life of dining on sheep and alarming the occasional virgin. The hero of the story is none other than Krak, the founder of the city. Handsome and clever, Krak fooled the dragon (nobody knows exactly how) into eating a tar-stuffed sheep, which subsequently exploded, to the delight of the local farm animals and young ladies. A six-legged metal statue of Smok Wawelski, that periodically breathes gas flames, stands outside the dragon's supposed former cave (daily Apr, Sept–Oct 10am–5pm; May–June 10am–6pm; July–Aug 10am–7pm).

collection of delightfully detailed and ornate saddles, several walls lined with crossbows, and a cellar containing cannons galore and reproductions of the banners captured at the Battle of Grunwald (see page 17).

Smok Wawelski, the fire-breathing dragon of legend

To the west on the other side of the courtyard wall is **Lost Wawel** (Zaginiony Wawel; Apr–Oct Tue–Fri 9.30–5pm, Mon 9.30am–1pm, Sat–Sun 10am–5pm, Nov–Mar Tue–Sat 9.30am–4pm, Sun 10am–4pm, free Sun in winter). This exhibition features archaeological finds from Wawel, as well as newer pieces, laid out in five rooms. The well-presented displays include medieval coins, remains of the castle's former royal kitchens and a Renaissance altar from Wawel Cathedral. The exhibition also has an exceptional multimedia show depicting how Wawel is believed to have looked between the 10th and 12th centuries.

At the far end of the castle grounds are the steps which lead down to the Dragon's Cave (see page 48) once said to be home to a fearsome dragon (see page 48). At the exit, Bronisław Chromy's metal sculpture of the dragon, **Smok Wawelski** surprisingly breathes real flames.

More information about Wawel can be found online at www.wawel.krakow.pl, or you can visit the **information centre** in the southwest corner of the complex daily Nov–Feb 9am–5pm, Mar, Oct 9am–6pm, Apr, Sept 9am–7pm, May, Aug 9am–8pm, and Jun–July, 9am–9pm; ticket office until 3.45pm in winter), which also has a gift shop, small post office and café.

BY THE RIVER WISŁA

Between Wawel and the Wisła is a small strip of parkland by the river known as **Bulwar Czerwieński** ㉑, which is popular in the summer with the locals as a place to lie in the sun and do nothing. If you're feeling active, you can follow the river on foot or by bike to Kazimierz. In the high season, boats moored by the river bank sell food and drink.

Directly across the water is the quirky **Manggha** (ul. Konopnickiej 26; http://manggha.pl; Tue–Sun Oct–June 10am–6pm, July–Sept 10am–8pm). Paid for by the late film director Andrzej Wajda, the swoop-roofed modern building is named for Feliks 'Manggha' Jasieński (1861–1929), a noted collector of Japanese art. Today it is a cultural centre hosting the Europe - Far East Gallery and temporary exhibitions, mainly of Oriental art. The museum also has a café and a pleasant terrace next to the river.

KAZIMIERZ

Kazimierz was founded in the 14th century as a town in its own right, a commercial rival to the German-dominated Kraków less than 1km (0.75 mile) to the north. Over the centuries, it has seen the best and worst of life. It's best-known as the one-time home of Kraków's thriving Jewish community, a fame that stems in part from the huge global success of the movie *Schindler's List*, much of which was filmed in and around Kazimierz. The delightfully scruffy district's contemporary reputation as a centre for all things cutting-edge, arty and bohemian has breathed new life into what was until recently a fairly uneventful place to visit. Kazimierz's unique mix of Jewish heritage and offbeat bars offers a refreshing alternative to the Old Town.

JEWISH KAZIMIERZ

At the time of the German invasion of 1939, Kraków had a rich 700-year-old Jewish tradition. Almost all of the city's 70,000 Jews (25 percent of the city's population) lived in Kazimierz. On 3 March 1941, the Germans began moving the Jewish population into the ghetto in Podgórze, just south of Kazimierz. By the time Kraków was liberated by the Red Army in January 1945, an entire Orthodox, Hassidic and secular culture had been destroyed; only about 2,000 Kraków Jews were still alive. Today, a revival of Jewish culture is under way in Kazimierz, and there's plenty to see. Information about the annual international Jewish festival can be found on page 94.

Shop and café fronts on ul. Szeroka

Around Ul. Szeroka

The nucleus of Kazimierz's Jewish revival can be found along **ul. Szeroka** ㉒, which is more of a square than a street. Here you'll find the main Jewish restaurants, as well as some good places to pick up books and information. At the southern end is the **Old Synagogue** ㉓ (Stara Synagoga; www.mhk.pl; Apr–Oct Mon 10am–2pm, Tue–Sun 9am–5pm; Nov–Mar Tue–Thu, Sat–Sun 9am–4pm, Mon 10am–2pm, Fri 10am–5pm; free on Mon). The earliest parts of Poland's oldest surviving synagogue date from the start of the 15th century, but many alterations have taken place over the centuries. The red-brick neo-Renaissance building is plain on the outside; the focus of interest is the interior, now a museum of Jewish heritage and culture, which provides a comprehensive primer to Jewish life in Kazimierz down the centuries.

North along ul. Szeroka is the **Remuh Synagogue** ㉔ (ul. Miodowa 24; http://krakow.jewish.org.pl; May–Sept Sun–Fri

9am–6pm, until 4pm Oct–Apr). Kraków's last working Orthodox synagogue was built in 1558 and has been completely renovated. This magnificent little building is next to the city's oldest remaining Jewish cemetery, which was replaced by the New Jewish Cemetery at the beginning of the 19th century. Among those laid to rest here is the renowned 16th-century writer and philosopher Rabbi Moses Isserles, known as Remuh, whose father founded the synagogue.

To the east on ul. Dajwór at No. 18 is the highly recommended **Galicia Jewish Museum** 25 (Galicja Żydowskie Muzeum; www.galiciajewishmuseum.org; daily 10am–6pm). The museum features an excellent permanent exhibition of contemporary photographs by the museum's founder Chris Schwartz of the remnants of Jewish culture in Galicia. It also runs a lively programme of cultural, musical and educational events, and its shop, gallery and information centre are good for finding out more about the city's Jewish heritage.

Plac Nowy

Until World War II, **Plac Nowy** 26, in the centre of Kazimierz and flanked by ul. Estery and ul. Warszauera, was the Jewish market. The ritual slaughterhouse rotunda at its centre recalls the area's former use. Nowadays, several of the best bars and cafés in Kraków are located here, attracting everyone from the area's colourful eccentrics to groups of youths feasting on kebabs.

East of the square, on ul. Kupa, is **Isaac Synagogue** (Synagoga Izaaka; Sun–Fri 9am–7pm), a 17th-century Judaic-Baroque masterpiece that was once famous for its stunning interior. Gutted by the Nazis, the synagogue has been restored to its former glory, but you can still come here and watch old films of Jewish life in the city before World War II. There is a Judaica store and kosher shop are on the premises.

North of Plac Nowy, at the junction of ul. Podbrzezie and ul. Miodowa, is the Reform Jewish congregation's **Tempel Synagogue** (Synagoga Templu; Sun–Fri 10am–6pm). Built in 1862, it was extended on both sides in 1924. It was one of the very few synagogues in Kazimierz that survived the Nazi regime virtually intact. The façade combines neo-Renaissance with Moorish influences, while the interior is beautifully ornamented with ornate stucco work, intricate red-and-gold polychromy, and a set of four circular stained-glass windows by the altar closet.

New Jewish Cemetery

Established at the beginning of the 19th century as a replacement for the overflowing Remuh Cemetery, the 19-hectare (47-acre) **New Jewish Cemetery** (Nowy Cmentarz Żydowski; Sun–Fri 9am–6pm or sunset), at the eastern end of ul. Miodowa (No. 55) beyond the railroad tracks, was the favoured place of burial for the well-off members of Kraków's Jewish community until the German invasion of the city in September 1939. The Nazis desecrated the cemetery, destroying most of the gravestones. Now partially restored, the cemetery is nevertheless overgrown. A few original gravestones remain, and fragments of broken headstones have been incorporated into the cemetery walls. There are also a number of memorials to entire families murdered during the Holocaust. A visit here is a haunting experience, and essential to anyone interested in Kraków's or Poland's Jewish history.

TWO MUSEUMS

Apart from Jewish heritage and hedonistic hangouts, Kazimierz also offers some other interesting attractions. The city's intriguing and informative **Ethnographic Museum** (Muzeum Etnograficzne; http://etnomuzeum.eu; Tue–Sun 10am–7pm; free on Sun) is

Inside the Ethnographic Museum, Kazimierz

located inside what was once Kazimierz's Town Hall on pl. Wolnica, southwest of pl. Nowy. Founded a century ago by the local teacher and folklore enthusiast Seweryn Udziela (1857–1937) as a way of preserving and promoting local folk culture within the region. Arranged over three floors, this extensive collection of folk art and culture from villages in the Kraków, Podhale and Silesian regions includes painted furniture, folk costumes and a small selection of the city's famous Christmas cribs (see page 90). The top floor is given over entirely to a stunning collection of folk art, including paintings, paper cuttings and crude wooden sculptures.

Kazimierz's other notable museum, a couple of streets to the northeast at ul. św. Wawrzyńca 15, is the **City Engineering Museum** (Muzeum Inżynierii Miejskiej; www.mim.krakow.pl; Tue 9am–4pm, Wed–Fri 9am–8pm, Sat–Sun 10am–8pm; free on Tue). It's really two museums in one. The main part is a motor museum, a fascinating collection of old cars, motorcycles, trams and other motor vehicles. Children especially will love the other part of the museum, the Fun and Science exhibition, which is located in a room adjoining the motor museum. This interactive hotchpotch of levers, pulleys and weights certainly lives up to its name. Some of the exhibits are decidedly whimsical, such as the cucumber that's had electrodes inserted into it; a voltameter

The Pauline Church, Kazimierz

proves that it generates an electric charge.

CATHOLIC KAZIMIERZ

There are several notable Catholic churches in the Kazimierz area. Of particular interest is the **Pauline Church** (Kościół Paulinów; ul. Skałeczna), located close to the river. The story of its founding is the stuff of legend: in 1079 or thereabouts the bishop of Kraków, Stanisław Szczepański, got himself into a bit of trouble with King Bolesław II the Bold, who accused him of treason and subsequently ordered his henchmen to hack him to pieces. Shortly after this, Bolesław's family fell under a terrible curse, and to make amends for what was believed to be retribution for the murder and to appease the spirit of poor Stanisław, this magnificent building was constructed. Well worth having a peep inside, the church is also the final resting place of the city's creative genius, Stanisław Wyspiański. Bishop Szczepański was eventually canonised and is buried in Wawel Cathedral (see page 45).

PODGÓRZE

Directly south of Kazimierz, across the Wisła, lies the sleepy suburb of Podgórze, once full of rundown shops and dirty factories, it is now experiencing the first stirrings of the kind of renaissance that has overtaken Kazimierz. Podgórze has one claim to fame: it was Kraków's ghetto during World War II. In 1941, between 3 and 21 March, the remaining Jewish population of Kazimierz was marched across the Powstańców Śląskich bridge and into 320 houses in the area around today's pl. Bohaterów Getta. A 3m (10ft) wall was built around the new ghetto. Until its final liquidation on 13–14 March 1943, the ghetto was home to about 20,000 Jews, of whom almost all were either worked to death or murdered at the nearby concentration camp at Płaszów (see page 62) or at Auschwitz (see page 72). Although there's not much to see, what remains is a poignant reminder of what the Nazis did in Poland between 1939 and 1944, and is worth taking the time to see.

GHETTO HEROES' SQUARE

Take tram No. 9 or 13 south over the Wisła and get off at the first stop, **Ghetto Heroes' Square** (pl. Bohaterów Getta). The square features a sculpture consisting of 70 scattered chairs made of bronze. Designed by Piotr Lewicki and Kazimierz Łatak, and called *Nowy Plac Zgody* (New Concordia Square, a reference to the square's former name, Concordia Square), the chairs are meant to recall a passage in a book by Tadeusz Pankiewicz (see page 59) describing the furniture left lying in the street after the ghetto's residents were rounded up for the final time in 1943.

In the far southwest corner of the square is the **Pharmacy Under Eagle** ㉗ (Apteka pod Orłem; www.

Famous survivor

The Kraków ghetto's most famous survivor is the film director Roman Polański. He's been one of the main contributors to the promotion of Podgórze as part of Kraków's increasingly popular tourist trail.

Pharmacy Under the Eagle

mhk.pl; Mon 10am–2pm, Tue–Sun 9am–5pm, closed every second Tue of the month; free on Mon), a branch of the Historical Museum. This was the site of the pharmacy, owned and run by Tadeusz Pankiewicz, the ghetto's only Gentile inhabitant (see box 59). The museum packs a powerful punch, featuring black-and-white photographs and some extraordinary films of ghetto life. A permanent exposition documents the Holocaust and Tadeusz Pankiewicz's life.

Heading south along ul. Lwowska is the first of two surviving pieces of **ghetto wall**. About two-thirds of the way along on the right-hand side is the smaller of the two remaining sections, commemorated with a small plaque. The second and much larger piece that once marked the ghetto's southern edge is hidden away to the left and behind the secondary school at ul. Limanowskiego 13.

SCHINDLER'S KRAKÓW

Backtrack the way you just came and head slightly to the east to **Oskar Schindler's Factory** ❷❽ (Fabryka Schindlera, ul. Lipowa 4; www.mhk.pl; Apr–Oct Mon 10am–4pm, Tue–Sun 9am–8pm; Nov–Mar Mon 10am–2pm, Tue–Sun 10am–6pm; free on Mon – limited number of tickets; last entry 90 mins before closing; advance booking essential at https://bilety.mhk.pl). This is the very place where Oskar Schindler first exploited and then protected and rescued more than 1,000 Jews of the Podgórze ghetto. The former administrative block is now a branch of the Historical Museum of the City of Kraków, with a permanent exhibition of Kraków under Nazi Occupation 1939–45. Schindler's actual office forms part of this 'Factory of Memory', which makes imaginative use of eyewitness accounts, documentary film and photographs, multimedia

⦿ TADEUSZ PANKIEWICZ

Tadeusz Pankiewicz (1908–93) was a Polish pharmacist and proprietor of the Apteka Pod Orłem (Pharmacy Under the Eagle) in Podgórze. In 1941 the Germans built the ghetto inside the area where his pharmacy was located. Declining an offer to relocate, he chose to live and work inside the ghetto along with his three Polish assistants. Besides his regular activities as a pharmacist, Pankiewicz gave sedatives to Jewish children to keep them quiet during Gestapo raids, and used his pharmacy as a secret meeting place for the ghetto's underground, as well as a place to hide Jews facing deportation to the death camps. After the war, Israel recognised him as Righteous Among the Nations, and he wrote a book, *The Kraków Ghetto Pharmacy*, about his experiences.

presentations and a symbolic Survivors' Ark, created from thousands of enamel pots similar to those made here during the ghetto years, to give the visitor the impression that they are taking a walk through the city in wartime, and facing the life or death decisions of those times.

The extraordinary events that took place here are widely known thanks to Steven Spielberg's film *Schindler's List*. Schindler was born to a wealthy and well-connected German-speaking family in the Czech town of Svitavy. He joined the Nazi Party in 1930 and moved to Kraków at the beginning of the war. Here he bought a bankrupt enamel factory from its Jewish owner and staffed it with cheap Jewish labour. Thanks to his charm and ability to conjure up desirable black-market goods, Schindler soon won over the SS.

In the summer of 1944 Schindler's workers were moved back to Płaszów, and it was at this time that he drew up his famous list of about 1,100 of the men and women working for him. He had them transferred to a weapons factory he established at his own cost in the town of Brünnlitz, close to where he was born. Three hundred Jewish women destined for Brünnlitz were accidentally sent to Auschwitz, and again Schindler used his connections to have them taken out (an act entirely unheard of in the Third Reich) and moved to the safety of Brünnlitz, where they were eventually liberated by the Red Army on 9 May 1945.

Schindler died in Frankfurt in 1974, and was buried in a Christian cemetery on Mount Zion in Jerusalem. His acts of bravery were even more impressive given that Poland was the only German-occupied country during World War II where helping a Jew was punishable by death.

Next door, the former factory floor has been transformed into the **Museum of Contemporary Art** ㉙ (MOCAK, Muzeum

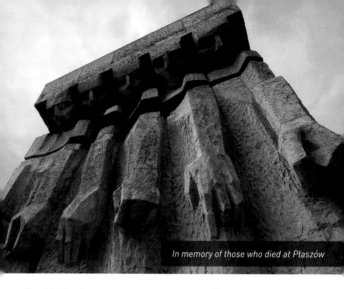

In memory of those who died at Płaszów

Sztuki Współczesnej w Krakowie; https://en.mocak.pl; Tue–Sun 11am–7pm; free on Tue), which stages a programme of temporary exhibitions and events in a clean, white space. The permanent collection in the basement includes some 4,000 works by Polish and international contemporary artists.

Another art centre worth visiting in Podgórze is **Cricoteka** ㉚ (ul.Nadwiślańska 2-4; www.cricoteka.pl; Tue–Sun 11am–7pm; free on Tue), a 'living archive' documenting the work and legacy of Tadeusz Kantor (1915–90). The avant-garde artist, reformer and director of the Cricot 2 theatre group was known for his revolutionary theatre productions. Located on the site of the former power station, with a façade of rusted metal and black mirror, it features a museum, theatre hall, archive, exhibition space, café and bookshop. Nearby at ul. Sienna 7/5 the **Gallery-Studio of Tadeusz Kantor**, (Fri–Mon noon–6pm; free) shows not only personal paraphernalia butt also temporary and workshops.

PŁASZÓW CONCENTRATION CAMP

Płaszów concentration camp opened in 1942 just west of Podgórze, on the site of two Jewish cemeteries destroyed by the Nazis. Now overgrown and almost completely destroyed, Płaszów rose to notoriety at the beginning of 1943 when it was taken over by the sadistic camp commander Amon Goeth. Shortly after Goeth's arrival, 6,300 residents of the Kraków ghetto were moved here, and the camp began its harshest phase, when it became the scene of unspeakable cruelty. Goeth is played by Ralph Fiennes in *Schindler's List*, and is seen in the film shooting unarmed prisoners from his balcony. Public torture and execution were almost daily occurrences at Płaszów. At the war's end, an unrepentant Amon Goeth was captured, tried, found guilty and hanged for his crimes on 13 September 1946, not far from Płaszów concentration camp.

Płaszów can be reached by taking tram No. 3, or 24 south a couple of stops from pl. Bohaterów Getta to Cmentarz Podgórski. Continue up the hill and take a right along ul. Jerozolimska. The camp entrance is by the second sign on the right. The main sights can be found at the top of the hill, up to the footpath on the left just after the cave. Of particular and startling interest is the Communist-built **monument**, dating from 1964, which commemorates all who died at the camp. Many of those who died at Płaszów were buried in the camp. Remember when you're here that you're walking on the site of a mass grave.

NOWA HUTA

The vast working-class district of Nowa Huta (New Steelworks), some 10km (6 miles) east of the city centre, was constructed soon after the end of World War II as an industrial centre that would help rebuild a nation flattened by both the Germans and the Allies during the war's six years. The Lenin Steelworks was the main development. Over the years the population of the new district grew rapidly, and today about 250,000 people live in Nowa Huta.

Paid for by the Soviet Union, Nowa Huta was constructed in the monumental socialist-realist architectural style typical of the Communist era. Nowa Huta is the only complete socialist-realist

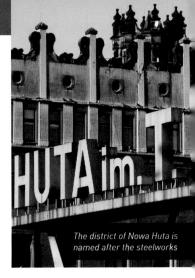

The district of Nowa Huta is named after the steelworks

town in the EU, and it's this architectural and political heritage that draws increasing numbers of visitors here.

SOCIALIST-REALIST SIGHTS

Trams No. 10 and 44 take about 30 minutes from the centre of Kraków to **Plac Centralny**, the central square of Nowa Huta and the starting point of a socialist-realist trip to the district. The square has been officially renamed in honour of the former US President Ronald Reagan. Finished in 1956, it's surrounded by huge, ostentatious concrete buildings whose style supposedly echoes Poland's great Baroque and Renaissance architecture. Five streets radiate from the square, of which the middle one, al. Róż, leads to an area in the northwest featuring most of the interesting and representative socialistrealist buildings.

Just past the park on the right heading up al. Róż is the **Museum of the History of the Nowa Huta Quarter** (Dzieje

Nowej Huty, os. Słoneczne 16; www.mhk.pl/oddzialy/dzieje-nowej-huty; Tue–Sun 9.30am–5pm, free on Tue) which stages changing exhibitions on the quarter's history and culture. From time to time, it also organises historic tours.

Heading northwest is **Sfinks** (os. Górali 5; www.kinosfinks.pl), a combined cinema and cultural centre of the type once seen all over the Communist world. Nearby is the **Teatr Ludowy** (os. Teatralne 34; www.ludowy.pl). The People's Theatre was built in 1955 and looks like a cross between a seaside pavilion and a Roman palace. Its long history of experimental productions includes *Romeo and Juliet* featuring rival punks and skinheads.

Across the street and impossible to miss, thanks to the large tank parked outside, is the **Museum of the Armed Act** (os. Górali 23; Muzeum Czynu Zbrojnego; Mon–Fri 10am–3pm; entrance by donation). It's a dark and dusty collection of memorabilia that celebrates Nowa Huta's military contributions to Polish history and the steelworkers who fought for their nation in battlefields all over the world. It contains photographs, uniforms and a disturbing series of models featuring scenes of Nazi atrocities and concentration-camp life.

Curious churches

Southeast of Nowa Huta is the tiny settlement of Mogiła, which is home to a remarkable pair of churches found on either side of ul. Klasztorna. Huge 13th-century St Wenceslas church in the Cistercian Abbey features intricate folk-art motifs on its walls and ceiling, while across the street 15th-century St Bartholomew's is one of few wooden churches in Kraków.

LORD'S ARK CHURCH

Head northwest along ul. Obrońców Krzyża where you will find Nowa Huta's **Lord's Ark Church** ③ (Kościół Arka Pana; www.arkapana.pl). It was constructed between

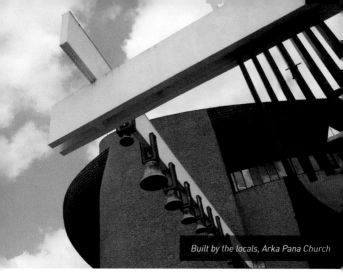

Built by the locals, Arka Pana Church

1967 and 1977 with no assistance from the officially atheist Communist regime. Instead, local people built it using nothing but their bare hands and limited tools. The method of construction may have been basic, but Wojciech Pietrzyk's design, built to resemble Noah's Ark, is nothing short of breathtaking. Inside the two-level structure, the tabernacle includes a tiny fragment of rutile brought from the moon by the crew of Apollo 11, and one of the many sculptures, *Our Lady of Armour*, was forged from 10kg (22lb) of shrapnel removed from Polish soldiers wounded at the World War II Battle of Monte Cassino, Italy. The imposing sculpture of Christ on the church's upper level breaks with convention, showing him blissfully flying to Heaven.

Some distance away, through leafy socialist-realist residential streets, is al. Solidarności, a long and stately road that leads from pl. Centralny to the entrance to the **Sendzimir** (formerly Lenin) **Steelworks**. On either side of the main gates are a pair of classic socialist-realist buildings known locally as the ***Doge*** after the Venetian palace they supposedly resemble. From here a No. 4 and 44 trams from the Kombinat stop run back to the city centre.

OUTLYING SIGHTS

Like any other large city, Kraków wasn't planned with tourists in mind. Accordingly there are a number of recommended sights spiralling out from the centre and into the depths of the city's suburbs, although most of the places to visit listed below are within easy walking distance of the Old Town. The sights are divided into eastern and western areas. Visiting the places in either area can be done in a few hours if you take everything in, with the exception of the zoo in the west and the Aviation Museum way out of the city centre in the east. The latter is virtually in Nowa Huta, and is worth visiting as part of a trip there.

TO THE EAST

Not far east of the railway station is **Celestat** (ul. Lubicz 16; www.mhk.pl/oddziały/celestat; Tue–Sat 10.30am–6pm). Also known as the History of Kraków's Marksmanship Guild, and one of the strangest museums in Kraków if not Poland, Celestat celebrates the history and culture of the city's **Marksmen Brotherhood** (Bractwo Kurkowe). Originating in medieval times, this was the Home Guard of its day. Brotherhoods all over Poland had the job of defending their respective cities. Made up of members of the merchant classes, the Marksmen Brotherhood favoured the lavish oriental dress style of the Sarmatians (see page 18), elected their own kings and had a silver cockerel as their mascot. The Kraków Marksmen Brotherhood, which is still very much alive and whose members can be found in attendance at major events in the city, used to crown new kings in St Mary's Basilica, an indication of its standing in the community. Nowadays, the outgoing king presents the silver cockerel to the new incumbent after Corpus Christi in June. The traditional ceremony is held on the Rynek.

The museum's collections include paintings of former kings, the story of Marksmen Brothers who perished at Auschwitz, and a 16th-century silver cockerel. Kraków's most famous Marksmen Brother was a cunning gentleman by the name of Marcin Oracewicz, who, so the legend goes, while rushing to defend the city during the Confederation of Bar (1768–72) forgot to bring his bullets. He therefore loaded his gun with his own buttons, of which one hit and mortally wounded the great Russian colonel, Panin. A small bust of Oracewicz stands outside the museum, and a plaque commemorating the shooting can be found on the east wall of the Barbican (see page 36), the supposed scene of this heroic deed.

Botanical Garden

A few minutes' walk southeast of Celestat is the **Botanical Garden** (Ogród Botaniczny Kraków; www.ogrod.uj.edu.pl; daily 9am–7pm; greenhouses close at 6pm and are not open on Fri). Founded in 1783 by the Jagiellonian University, this is the oldest botanical garden in Poland. Their 10

In the Botanical Garden

City park

To the west of the city centre is the Błonia, a lovely city park covering 120 hectares (296 acres) of meadow. It's particularly favoured by Kraków's dog-walking and jogging communities.

hectares (25 acres) include herb gardens, hothouses, ponds with water plants, a wonderfully fragrant collection of roses, as well as pleasant, tree-lined paths. A visit here makes a nice break from tramping the city's streets. The gardens also play host to a series of classical music concerts during the summer months.

Polish Aviation Museum

Out of the city centre just west of Nowa Huta is the **Polish Aviation Museum ㉜** (Muzeum Lotnictwa Polskiego; al. Jana Pawła II 39; www.muzeumlotnictwa.pl; Tue–Sun 9am–5pm; free on Tue), a better-than-average collection of flying machines and other aeronautical memorabilia inside a stylish glass building. Among the antique wooden aircraft and piles of rusty Soviet-era MIG fighters are a few things that really stand out, including one of the world's few remaining Spitfires in perfect condition. To get there take tram No. 4, 10, 44 or 52 to Muzeum Lotnictwa stop.

TO THE WEST

A 15-minute walk northwest of the Old Town along ul. Karmelicka takes you to Poland's only museum given over entirely to the art of photography, the **History of Photography Museum** (Muzeum Historii Fotografii; ul. Józefitów 16; www.mhf.krakow.pl). Look past the museum's small size and uninspiring collection of old cameras to the permanent display of old pictures of the city.

A recommended short itinerary for those on foot after leaving the photography museum starts by heading south through the

5-hectare (12-acre) **Park Krakowski**, which was laid out in 1887 by Stanisław Rehman and was once the location of an outdoor theatre. The park is scattered with a few interesting modern sculptures. There are other sculptures further down the street, outside the **University of Science and Technology** (Politechnika Krakowska; al. Mickiewicza 30). Ceramic figures of miners and steelworkers grace either side of the main entrance to the building. The work of Jan Raszka (1871–1945), they appear to be typically heroic characters from the days of Communism, but they actually predate that era, having been produced in 1935.

National Museum

Immediately to the south lies one of the highlights of the city if not Poland, the **National Museum** ③ (Muzeum Narodowe; al. 3 Maja 1; http://mnk.pl; Tue–Sat 10am–6pm, Sun 10am–4pm). There are three floors of galleries. Suits of armour, swords, firearms and medals are among over 2,000 military articles on display in the Arms and Uniforms Gallery. The Gallery of Decorative Art has a large collection of Polish and Western European decorative arts and crafts from medieval times to the early 1900s. The Gallery of 20th-century Polish Art contains over 400 works, and

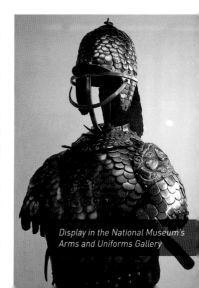

Display in the National Museum's Arms and Uniforms Gallery

includes excellent coverage of the Young Poland (Młoda Polska) art movement. The museum also hosts high-quality temporary exhibitions, and there's a good bookshop and a small café. Don't miss the opportunity to see Leonardo da Vinci's *Lady with an Ermine*, which belongs to the Czartoryski Museum (currently under renovation) and is temporarily displayed in the main building. Interestingly, it is one of only three of da Vinci's oil canvases left in the world. Within walking distance from the main building, is another branch of the museum, the **Europeum** (same hours as National Museum). Located in a 17th-century granary building at Pl. Sikorskiego 6, the Europeum houses the museum's permanent exhibition of European art, include Catalan medieval Madonnas, Jan Gossaert's (also known as Jan Mabuse) *Man of Sorrows*, Luca Giordano's *The Flight into Egypt*a and Rembrandt's *Landscape with the Good Samaritan*. On your way to the Europeum, it's worth taking a look at the interesting **Stain Glass Museum and Workshop** (Pracownia i Muzeum Witrażu, al. Krasinskiego 23; https://muzeumwitrazu.pl; guided tours only, Tue–Sat noon–5pm in English).

Salt sanatorium

Since the middle of the 19th century, when salt baths were first touted for their healing potential, Wieliczka has also enjoyed the benefits of a sanatorium. Today the mines' underground chambers are still used as a location for the treatment of respiratory illnesses, particularly asthma, and allergies.

Kraków Zoo

Much further out into the depths of Kraków's leafy suburbs is **Kraków Zoo and Zoological Gardens** (Miejski Park i Ogród Zoologiczny w Krakowie; ul. Kasy Oszczędności Miasta Krakowa 14; www.zoo-krakow.pl; daily 9am–7pm). You'll find the usual collection of big cats and frisky

Chapel of St Kinga, Wieliczka Salt Mine

monkeys, as well as a small zoo made especially for children. The zoo is surrounded by the city's Zoological Garden, a popular place for picnics away from the noise of the metropolis. To get there, take a westbound bus No. 134 from the stop just west of the National Museum. The journey time is about 20 minutes.

EXCURSIONS

Each of the following four destinations can be explored in a day. Two of these, Tarnów and Zakopane, also provide an opportunity to expand on a Kraków city break. Tarnów's immediate charm lies in its superb Old Town, but its other points of interest, including museums and a rich Jewish heritage, justify a longer visit if you have the time. The same can be said for Zakopane, with its rapidly expanding nightlife scene and year-round opportunities for outdoor activities in the magnificent Tatra Mountains.

WIELICZKA SALT MINES

Twenty million years ago the area around Kraków was covered by sea. When the water receded, a large deposit of salt was left under the ground, which has been a source of wealth in the region since the Stone Age. In the 13th century, large-scale rock salt extraction began, and mines sprang up (or rather, down) everywhere. The Unesco-listed mines at **Wieliczka** ㉞ (www.kopalnia.pl; daily for guided tours only: daily Apr–Oct 7.30am–7.30pm, Nov–Mar 8am–5pm) are 10km (6 miles) southeast of Kraków, accessible by train from the main station, or bus 304 from ul. Kurniki opposite Galeria Krakowska or by minibus leaving from the parking area at the corner of ul. Worcella and ul. Pawia.. The tour visits 20 chambers ranging from 64m (210ft) to 135m (443ft), though the nine levels of the mine burrow down to 327m (1,075ft). Over the centuries, the subterranean chambers have been carved and decorated by miners. Highlights include **St Anthony's Chapel**, created in the 17th century, and the mines' 23,000 cu m (812,200 cu ft) masterpiece, the **Chapel of St Kinga**, with beautiful carvings of New Testament scenes. Visits end at a combined restaurant and gift shop before you ascend to ground level in a lift.

AUSCHWITZ

About 60km (37 miles) west of Kraków is the small and seemingly insignificant town of **Oświęcim**, better-known to the world under its German name, **Auschwitz** ㉟. This was the site of two Nazi concentration camps: Auschwitz I and Auschwitz II (Birkenau). More than 1.1 million people were murdered in the camps, and 90 percent of them were Jewish.

Auschwitz is by far the most popular day trip from Kraków. Each year, about half a million people make the journey here to try to comprehend the incomprehensible. Both camps are frightening,

Auschwitz II (Birkenau)

terrible and deeply disturbing places to visit. Think hard about what you're expecting to get from Auschwitz before you go there.

Auschwitz I (tel: 033 844 80 99; www.auschwitz.org; daily Dec 7.30am–2pm, Jan, Nov until 3pm, Feb until 4pm, Mar, Oct until 5pm, Apr–May and Sept until 6pm, June–Aug until 7pm; advance booking essential at https://visit.auschwitz.org; children under 12 should not watch the introductory film, though they are admitted; entrance to the camps is free, there is a charge for the introductory film and for guided tours) was the first camp to open, in 1940. Pass through the gates bearing the infamous maxim *Arbeit Macht Frei* (Work Sets You Free) and enter a place of unspeakable wickedness. Developed on the grounds of an abandoned Polish army camp, Auschwitz I remains almost intact, looking more like an old holiday resort than the site of some of the worst crimes ever committed. The red-brick barracks are dedicated to the nationalities who died here. Other sights include the wall where inmates were shot; a harrowing collection of suitcases, shoes, other personal possessions and even human hair; the (recreated) ovens where the dead were turned to ash; and, just next to the ovens, the gallows where camp commandant Rudolf Höss was executed in 1947.

Three kilometres (2 miles) away is the second camp, Auschwitz II, or **Birkenau**. Opened in 1942, Birkenau became the main site of the extermination of the Jewish race after the Final Solution was approved by the Nazis. Trains from all over Europe could go right into the camp. On arrival, a selection of prisoners took place – three-quarters of all new arrivals were immediately taken away and murdered in the gas chambers. With little in the way of exhibits, Birkenau captures the sheer terror of Auschwitz more than the original camp.

Colourful merchant houses in the Old Town of Tarnów

Getting to Auschwitz is easy, with plenty of buses leaving from the main bus station each day, and there are also a few trains. Tours from Kraków are plentiful, and are worth considering, although prices tend to be high. People visiting Auschwitz independently should buy the excellent brochure from the small kiosk on the right as you enter the main doors of Auschwitz I.

TARNÓW

Located 80km (50 miles) to the east of Kraków, the small town of **Tarnów** ❸⓺ boasts an almost perfectly preserved Old Town of impressive Gothic, Baroque and Renaissance architecture. Scratch the surface and you'll also find reminders of a rich history involving Jews, Roma and many others. The town is just one hour from Kraków by express train, and the best bits can be seen comfortably in a day if you start early. However, there are plenty of attractions to warrant an overnight stay.

Rynek and the Old Town

Tarnów's Old Town retains its original layout of a raised central area of latticed streets with a grand market square (Rynek) at its centre and a lower, oval-shaped encompassing loop reached by a series of stairways. The Old Town began life in the 14th century, although most of what now stands dates from later periods. With its magnificent merchant houses, fine museums and other notable sights, the Old Town should be your first port of call.

The Old Town's crowning glory is the **Rynek**, a wide-open plaza surrounded by fine Renaissance houses. The Rynek's centre-piece is the 15th-century **Town Hall** (Ratusz), an elaborate yellow Gothic and Renaissance building with attics topping its roof and a 30m (100ft) tower. Inside is the **Tarnów District Museum** (Muzeum Okręgowe w Tarnowie; www.muzeum.tarnow.pl; Oct–Apr Thu 9am–5pm, Tue, Wed, Fri 9am–3pm, May–Sept Tue, Thu

9am–5pm, Wed, Fri 9am–3pm, Sat–Sun 10am–4pm). Among the highlights are Poland's best collection of 18th-century Sarmatian portraits (see page 18) and a celebration of the life of the soldier and patriot Józef Bem (1794–1850), who was born in Tarnów. During the summer, the Rynek comes alive with outdoor cafés, and is a great place to sit and socialise.

In the northeast corner of the Rynek is the **cathedral** (Katedra). Dating from the 14th century, with later additions made in the 15th and 19th centuries, the now mostly neo-Gothic red-brick building has a number of points of interest, both inside and out. Of particular note are the fine 16th-century monuments to the Tarnowski family, who once owned the town, and the 72m (236ft) high tower, visible throughout the town and forming a useful landmark. Immediately behind the Cathedral is the **Diocesan Museum** (Muzeum Diecezjalne; www.muzeum.diecezja.tarnow. pl; Tue–Fri 10am–noon and 1–3pm, till 2pm Sat–Sun; free), which has a collection of religious art from the 15th century onwards.

Jewish life

At its height, Tarnów's Jewry was a thriving secular and religious community of both Orthodox and Hasidic Jews, many of whom held distinguished positions in the town. Sadly, the largest reminder of Jewish life today is the massive Jewish graveyard near the junction of ul. Słoneczna and al. Matki Bożej Fatimskiej.

Jewish Tarnów

Directly east of the Rynek in a part of the Old Town now populated by a number of interesting little bars is the area where the majority of the town's Jews lived, until the Holocaust obliterated a people that from the 15th century until June 1944 made up around 40 percent of Tarnów's population.

The part of the Old Town between ul. Żydowska and

ul. Wekslarska still features a handful of Jewish houses with their original *mezuzah* boxes in the doorways – a haunting reminder of what used to be. Heading east along ul. Żydowska on the left is a massive, forlorn-looking **bimah**, all that's left of the town's 17th-century synagogue after the Nazis burnt it down on the evening of 9 November 1939. Heading further in the same direction out of the

Tarnów's Cathedral

Old Town, at pl. Bohaterów Getta, is the 1904 **Moorish Jewish Bath House**, now a gruesome footnote in the town's history – it was from which the Nazis first deported local people – 753 convicts from the prison, five of them Jews – to Auschwitz.

Other Highlights

There are a number of exceptional sights within easy walking distance of the Old Town. Between the railway station and the Old Town at ul. Krakowska 10 is the **Ethnographic Museum** (Muzeum Etnograficzne; www.muzeum.tarnow.pl; same hours as the Tarnów District Museum), inside a gorgeous wooden cottage. It's crammed with colourful folk costumes and art from the region, as well as what's claimed to be the only permanent display on Roma culture in Europe. The Roma (Gypsies) have been living in Tarnów since the 15th century and are still represented by around 200 individuals.

In the south, not too far from one another, are two fine wooden churches. Closest to the centre on ul. Panny Marii is **St Mary's Church** (Kościół Najświętszej Marii Panny). This diminutive 15th-century larch building is often open, rewarding visitors with a glimpse inside a typical Polish parish church, typified by colourful painted flowers on the ceiling. A little further south on ul. Tuchowska is the **Holy Trinity Church** (Kościół św. Trójcy), a 16th-century Gothic building notable for the painting *Throne of Grace*, depicting God with six fingers on his left hand, signifying the number of days taken to create the Earth.

THE TATRAS

The highest section of the Carpathian mountain range, the Tatras cover an area that takes in the region immediately south of Zakopane and stretching into neighbouring Slovakia. The spectacular karst peaks, dense pine forests and clear lakes make up one of the few areas of pristine wilderness in Europe, where eagles fly and brown bears and chamois roam. The Tatras are a hugely popular summertime destination for Polish hikers, while in the winter, skiers come to enjoy the slopes dotted around Zakopane and take the cable car to the 1,000m (3,300ft) runs on the Kasprowy Wierch mountain.

Inside a small hut next to the Rondo Kuźnickie is the **Tatra National Park Information Centre** (Rondo Jana Pawła II; www. tpn.pl; Mon–Sat 7.30am–3.30pm), where you'll find more information on things to see and do in the Tatras. They also sell maps and guidebooks in English.

ZAKOPANE

Nestled in the dip of a valley between the hillside hamlet of Gubałówka and the northernmost tip of the Tatra Mountains,

Stunning views in the Tatras

the small wooden town of **Zakopane** ㊲ is renowned throughout Poland as both the nation's winter capital and as a place to come for rest and relaxation. It was originally a village of the Gorals (Górale), a small ethnic group of mountain people, and became a popular destination thanks to the tireless promotion of 19th-century doctor Tytus Chałubiński. Just 110km (68 miles) south of Kraków, Zakopane and its Goral culture makes for an interesting day trip at any time of year, and provides a more substantial base for those looking for adventures in the great outdoors.

A 10-minute walk southwest from the railway and bus stations along ul. Kościuszki brings you to the town's main street, **ul. Krupówki**. All three main sights can be found by turning right at this junction. Down the hill on the left at ul. Krupówki 10 is the **Tatra Museum** (Muzeum Tatrzańskie; www.muzeum tatrzanskie.com.pl; Tue–Sat 9am–5pm, May–Sept, Sun

9am–3pm), where you can find out more about the region and its mountain culture. Housed inside a classic wooden house, the museum is spread over two floors. Exhibits include traditional costumes, old farming implements and recreations of the interiors of local homes as they were in the 19th century. Unfortunately, there's little information in English.

Turn left at the end of the street and just on the right is the charming and diminutive **St Mary of Częstochowa Church** (Kościół Matki Boskiej Częstochowskiej; daily 8.30am–4pm). It was built entirely of wood between 1847 and 1851, and is Zakopane's oldest standing house of worship. The interior is decorated with folk art, but the church is perhaps more famous for its graveyard. This is the final resting place of the great and the good of the town, including Helena

⊙ HELENA MARUSARZÓWNA

Of the many Polish World War II heroines, perhaps none is more deserving of remembrance than Helena Marusarzówna. Born in Zakopane in 1918, the year Poland regained its independence, the teenage girl from the mountains won seven Polish skiing championships between 1936 and the outbreak of World War II. Barely into her twenties, she joined the Polish underground and begun smuggling mail and refugees over the Tatra Mountains and into Hungary. In March 1940, she was captured by the Hungarian police and handed over to the Gestapo, who tortured her on several occasions before they executed her the following year. She didn't give away a single secret, and was posthumously awarded the Virtuti Militari and the Cross of Bravery. She is buried in the graveyard of St Mary of Częstochowa Church.

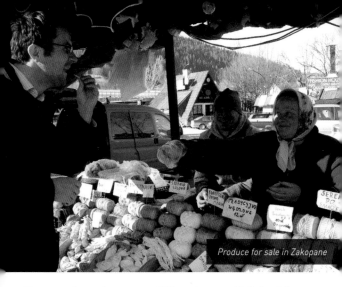

Produce for sale in Zakopane

Marusarzówna (see page 80), a former Polish skiing champion and resistance activist executed by the Nazis during World War II.

A little further up on the same side of the road is the town's first building in the wooden Zakopane Style. The **Zakopane Style Museum** (Muzeum Stylu Zakopiańskiego; www.muzeum tatrzanskie.pl; Wed–Sat 9am–5pm, Sun 9am–3pm) is located inside the Willa Koliba, built in 1894 by Stanisław Witkiewicz and featuring rooms set out as they were when the building was constructed. At the top of the stairs are some fine carved wooden pieces in an almost Art Deco style, plus a large collection of paintings by Witkiewicz's son, known to the world as Witkacy (1885–1939), all painted under the influence of different drugs (the drug in question being recorded on each canvas along with the signature), and collectively far more infamous than they are accomplished.

Shop for hand-painted gifts

WHAT TO DO

ENTERTAINMENT

With numerous theatres, music venues, cinemas, bars, clubs and festivals catering to every taste imaginable, Poland's unofficial cultural capital has an enormous capacity to keep its visitors entertained. You'll find all of the excellent official Kraków tourist information centres have many branches, but a centrally placed one is at ul. św. Jana 2 (tel: 012 354 27 25; daily 9am–7pm) full of information about cultural and entertainment events throughout the city. Tickets for a night at the opera or cinema are not expensive (30–140zł and less than 30zł respectively).

THEATRE

Theatre performances are almost always in Polish, so check to see if simultaneous translations are available. The **Stary Teatr** (ul. Jagiellońska 1; tel: 012 422 80 20; www.stary.pl) was Poland's first ever playhouse. It focuses mostly on classic and lavish theatre productions from Poland and abroad. Other theatres of note include the **Bagatela** (ul. Karmelicka 6; tel: 012 422 66 77; www.bagatela.pl), Kraków's leading home of musical theatre and light entertainment; the fabulous **Juliusz Słowacki Theatre** (pl. św. Ducha 1; tel: 012 424 45 28; http://teatrwkrakowie.pl/), which prides itself on both grand theatre and the occasional opera; and the **Groteska Puppet, Mask & Actor Theatre** (ul. Skarbowa 2; tel: 012 633 37 62/12 623 79 59; www.groteska.pl), which preserves the very best traditions in Eastern European puppet and experimental theatre for both children and adults. Also worth a mention is Nowa Huta's typically offbeat, working-class **Teatr Ludowy** (see page 64).

CLASSICAL AND OPERA

Especially during the summer, when many orchestras take to the streets and parks of the city, Kraków comes alive with classical concerts, opera and, particularly in the city's many churches, choral music.

The **Kraków Filharmonia** (ul. Zwierzyniecka 1; tel: 012 619 87 33; www.filharmonia.krakow.pl) is located just west of the Old Town in a rather ugly-looking building that belies what takes place inside. As well as the orchestra's own weekly symphony concerts and performances by visiting international soloists, the Filharmonia plays a leading role in the musical life of the city with performances in historical spaces and work with young people.

The **Opera Krakowska** (ul. Lubicz 48; tel: 012 296 61 ½; www.opera.krakow.pl) concentrates on productions of classical operas. Kazimierz's smaller and less well-known **Krakowska Opera Kameralna** (ul. Miodowa 15; tel: 012 430 66 06; www.kok.art.pl) is the place to head for if you're looking to

---

✿ FLOWER ETIQUETTE

Giving flowers (kwiaty) in Poland comes with a sophisticated set of rules that if not followed can lead to potentially embarrassing situations, especially among the older generation. The most important things to know are that you should always give an odd number of flowers (even numbers are reserved for solemn occasions) and that they should be given with the left hand. You should give your fiancée red flowers, her mother pink, and stay clear of anything yellow, the traditional colour of envy. Chrysanthemums are for funerals only. Last but not least, carnations represent communism, so be careful who you give these to.

Juliusz Słowacki Theatre stages grand theatre and opera

see some traditional folk music performances, Yiddish songs and the puppet opera theatre.

CINEMA

Poland has an enviable cinematic tradition, and the Poles are dedicated movie-goers. Three cinemas worth attending for their individual merits are **ARS** (ul. św. Tomasza 11; tel: 012 421 41 99; www.ars.pl) in the Old Town, which caters to a mostly mainstream audience; **Kino Pod Baranami** (Rynek Główny 27; tel: 012 423 07 68; www.kinopodbaranami.pl), a fine cinema keeping the arthouse and independent cinema scene in the city alive; and the immense **Kraków Plaza IMAX** (al. Pokoju 44; tel: 012 290 90 90; www.cinema-city.pl), east of the city centre and reached on trams No. 1, 12, 14 and 22. Galeria Kazimierz (see also page 92) has another fine **Cinema City** multiplex, catering to the needs of the average

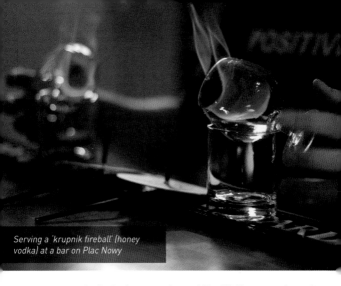

Serving a 'krupnik fireball' (honey vodka) at a bar on Plac Nowy

popcorn-fuelled, cinema-going public. All films are shown in their original language with Polish subtitles.

NIGHTLIFE

Poland's best nightlife city, Kraków has a fine choice of bars, clubs and live music venues. The fact that the city centre is so small makes pub-crawling particularly attractive, especially when there appears to be a kebab shop between every drinking hole. Two cultural differences worth noting are that a Polish cocktail bar is in fact an ice-cream parlour, and, particularly in the areas just outside the Old Town, many places that call themselves nightclubs are in fact brothels. A red light usually gives the game away.

BARS

Kazimierz has by far the finest selection of bars, with **Alchemia** (ul. Estery 5; tel: 012 421 22 00; http://alchemia.com.pl), an arty, candlelit affair, being the most talked about. Service is at the bar, and likely to be friendly rather than fast. Alchemia also has its own performance space, with bands, films and theatre all programmed. Across the street, **Le Scandale** (pl. Nowy 9; tel: 012 430 68 55), serves great cocktails amid a brighter atmosphere. The café that could claim to have started the Kazimierz revival, **Singer** (ul. Izaaka 1; tel: 012 292 06 22), is rightly still many people's favourite. From the tables fashioned from old sewing machine stands (hence the name) to the sheer diversity of people who come here to drink, it sums up the particular charm of Kazimierz. Also worth mentioning are **Tajemniczy Ogród** (Plac Nowy 9; tel: 012 430 67 76; http://tajemniczy.com.pl) and **Pub Stajnia** (ul. Izaaka 7/1; tel: 012 423 72 02; www.pubstajnia.pl).

During the balmy summer months, the streets, squares and many of the hidden courtyards of the Old Town also fill up with chattering tables full of people out for a little al fresco drinking, creating one of the most pleasant and relaxed drinking experiences in the city. Or you could make your way down to the river under Wawel Hill, where floating bars and restaurants cater to a range of pockets. One of the more upmarket is **Aquarius** (Bulwar Czerwieński; tel: 12 427 20 03; www.aquariuskrakow.pl).

The nearby **Someplace Else** (ul. Powiśle 7; tel: 012 662 10 00; www.krakow.someplace-else.pl) is inside the Sheraton Hotel, so expect a Western bill at the end of a session.

Right in the Old Town, the **Wódka Café Bar** (ul. Mikołajska 5; tel: 012 422 32 14) is a little place when you can sample shots of differenl flavoured Polish

> **In your pocket**
>
> For a thorough and up-to-date investigation of the city's nightlife, pick up a copy of *Kraków In Your Pocket* when you're in town.

vodkas, including horseradish, chilli and pepper ones if you're feeling adventurous.

CLUBS

Kraków's nightlife tempts everyone from rowdy stag parties to the older generation out for a few shots of vodka and a good old knees-up. **Frantic** (ul. Szewska 5; tel: 012 423 04 83; www.frantic.pl) caters to people who look like they fell out of a fashion magazine, so dress nicely and they may well let you in.

More mainstream, and frequently showcasing live bands, **Stalowe Magnolie** (ul. św. Jana 15; tel: 012 422 84 72; http://stalowemagnolie.pl) is justifiably as popular with local students as the visitors who relish its vaulted ceilings and fin-de-siècle interior.

Next door, **Cień** (ul. św. Jana 15; tel: 012 422 21 77; www.cienklub.com) is packed with B-list beauties and has a tight face control. Cień guarantees a good night out and the chance to mix with people who drive very expensive black cars.

A perennial favourite is **Prozak** (pl. Dominikański 6; http://prozakdwazero.pl/), although drinks are overpriced.

For a gay-friendly atmosphere, make for the long-standing **Cocon club** (ul. Gazowa 21; tel: 503 77 38 44; www.klub-cocon.pl), where a maze of rooms, large and small, hosts different kinds of dance music, with chill-out spaces and a heated garden for smokers. Occasionally, you'll find theatre, karaoke and even ballroom dancing here, too.

SHOPPING

Kraków offers a disparate mix of retail options, ranging from vast new shopping malls to shops selling religious souvenirs or 1960s bric-a-brac. The main shopping areas are the Old Town, given over almost exclusively to the sale of expensive designer clothes and cheap souvenirs, and Kazimierz, which is the place to go for antiques and second-hand bargains.

SPECIALITY SHOPPING

The area in and around the Rynek Główny provides ample opportunities for picking up souvenirs, including amber, stuffed Wawel dragons, fake swords and many other treats faux-medieval and modern. As well as selling this sort of thing, the ground floor of the **Cloth Hall** (see page 29) has some authentic local linen and folk art, including locally-made carved wooden sculptures of religious and agricultural scenes, and Góral leatherwear and knitwear from the highlands.

Shopping in the Cloth Hall

The area running north–south east of the Rynek is the best place to pick up such things as flashing Jesus paintings, priests' outfits, holy wine and more. The quirky **Arkos** (pl. Mariacki 5; tel: 012 421 86 61; http://mariacki.com/en/shop/ ; Mon–Fri 10am–6pm, Sat 10am–2pm) is perhaps the most representative of these shops.

Local arts and crafts make excellent gifts and souvenirs, but it can be difficult to know what's what and whether you're getting the real thing. Try the excellent shop **Krakuska Sztuka Ludowa** (ul. Szewska 9; tel: 012 430 21 04; Mon–Fri 10am–8pm, Sat 11am–8pm, Sun until 6pm), with a wide choice of quality crafts, including tapestries, embroidery, Bolesławiec ceramics, painted glass, leather products and folk costumes.

Amber is the country's national stone, and jewellery made from either amber or silver, or both, often represents very good value. As well as traditional designs, many shops sell excellent

⊙ CHRISTMAS CRIBS

Christmas cribs *(szopka)* are a speciality of Kraków. They began appearing in the 19th century, the work of local craftsmen with time on their hands during the slow autumn months. Large (often 2m/6.5ft), brightly coloured and ornately decorated portable theatres depicting the Nativity scene, these unique creations have become one of the symbols of the city. In 1937 the first competition was held in the city to choose the best, an event that continues to this day. During the morning of the first Thursday of December, the best Christmas cribs are displayed in the Rynek between the Cloth Hall and St Mary's. The winners are later taken to the Ethnographic Museum in Kazimierz (see page 54); the rest are sold on the spot.

contemporary jewellery by Polish designers. Try **Mikołajczyki Amber** (tel: 012 428 50 86; www.boruni.pl; daily 9am–9pm), in the Cloth Hall and other locations around the city.

Keep in mind that in Poland it's illegal to export any items more than 50 years old without an official permit. Any reputable antique shop will help you with this.

Souvenir axes on sale in Zakopane

MARKETS AND MALLS

Kraków's markets range from the sublime to the ridiculous. The former is represented by the wonderful Kazimierz market **Plac Nowy** (Plac Nowy; www.placnowy.pl; daily 8am–3pm), which offers different goods on different days, from tacky clothing (Sun) to the superb bric-à-brac market held every Saturday. The two central markets, selling cheap Chinese imports as well as a good choice of local cheese, meat and flowers, are the **Hala Targowa** (Plac Targowy, ul Grzegórzecka; www.unitarg.krakow.pl; hall daily 6am–5pm; outdoor market Sat 6am–2pm, Sun 6am-1.30pm), with probably the best grilled sausages (kielbasa) sold from the van, and **Stary Kleparz** (Rynek Kleparski; www.starykleparz.com; Mon–Fri 7am–6pm, Sat till 3pm, Sun 8am–3pm), which has been in business for hundreds of years, and is great fun and an excellent source of flowers, sausages and, in the autumn, local mushrooms.

Malls are sprouting up everywhere and are a welcome refuge during the harsh winter months especially. The two heavyweights are **Galeria Kazimierz** (ul. Podgórska 34; www.galeriakazimierz.pl; Mon–Sat 10am–9pm, Sun 10am–8pm), **Galeria Krakowska** (ul. Pawia 5; www.galeriakrakowska.pl; Mon–Sat 9am–10pm, Sun 10am–9pm), next to the railway station, and the recently opened Serenada (al. Gen. T. Bora-Komorowskiego 41; Mon–Sun 10am–9pm; www.centrumserenada.pl). Note that as of 2018, all bigger shops are required by law to be closed at least two Sun of each month (smaller ones may stay open if their owners themselves decide to stand behind the counter).

SPORTS AND ACTIVITIES

Swimming. The city has two excellent places in which to swim. **Park Wodny** (ul. Dobrego Pasterza 126; tel: 012 616 31 90; www.parkwodny.pl; daily 8am–10pm) is a massive complex with water slides as well as beauty facilities and a decent café. The smaller **Klub Sportowy Korona** (ul. Kalwaryjska 9–15; tel: 012 656 13 68; www.korona.krakow.pl) has a 25m (82ft) pool.

Ice skating. The two ice rinks at **Lodowisko Krakowianka** (ul. Siedleckiego 7; tel: 012 421 13 17; http://cracovia.pl) are open to the public when the local ice-hockey team isn't using them. There are no such restrictions at the winter-only rink at the open-air rink in the Jordan Park (al. 3 Maja 11atel: 697 008 340; http://lodowisko-krakowskieblonia.pl).

Paintballing. With Kraków's blossoming as a top stag party destination, visitors can now enjoy running about in a forest and shooting each other with coloured paint courtesy of a number of specialist companies, of which **Crazy Stag** (www.crazystag.com) is one of the most popular.

Golf. Golf is available at two courses. The **Kraków Valley Golf & Country Club** (ul Paczółtowice 328, Krzeszowice; tel: 012 258 60 00; www.krakow-valley.com) offers 18 holes some 40km (25 miles) west of the city, while in the opposite direction the more upmarket **Royal Kraków Golf & Country Club** (ul. Ochmanów 124, Podłęże; tel: 012 281 91 70; www. krakowgolf. pl) provides nine holes 18km (11 miles) away in the splendid Royal Jagiellonian Hunting Grounds.

Hiking. The vast countryside of Poland is ideal for leisurely walking and more athletic hiking. One of the best areas for both, especially for serious hikers, are the High Tatra Mountains around Zakopane (see page 78).

Skiing. Winter sports equipment is available in abundance in Zakopane, both for sale and hire, especially in the main street, ul. Krupówki. Ski rental costs from between about 50zł and 100zł per day. Renting a snowboard costs about 50zł a day. One hour with a ski instructor costs anything from 100zł up.

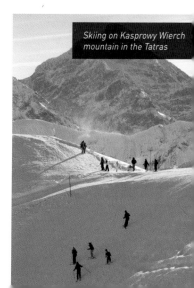

Skiing on Kasprowy Wierch mountain in the Tatras

Football. Kraków's two professional football teams are **Cracovia** (ul. Kałuży 1; www.cracovia.pl) and **Wisła Krakow** (ul. Reymonta 22; www.wisla.krakow. pl). Both teams play in the country's top league, Ekstraklasa. Be warned: Polish football crowds can get be rowdy at times.

FESTIVALS

Kraków has a reputation as a city of great festivals, hosting more than 100 each year). Among the outstanding events are: International Festival of Independent Cinema, **Netia Off Camera** (www.offcamera.pl) in April/May; the colossal **Jewish Festival of Culture** (www.jewishfestival.pl), held in Kazimierz and the Old Town from the end of June to the beginning of July each year; September's delightfully different **Sausage Dog Parade**; and the ancient pagan tradition of **Wianki** on St John's Day (24 June), when the young ladies of the city float candlelit wreaths down the Wisła River near Wawel, light bonfires and everyone drinks lots of alcohol. Then there are **classical concerts** inside the nearby salt mines in Wieliczka, **the Sacrum Profanum 20th-century music festival** (www.sacrumprofanum.com), a superb **jazz festival** and much more than space here allows. You will find more informationin the monthly magazine *Karnet*, available in hotels and kiosks around the city (www.karnet.krakow.pl).

CHILDREN'S KRAKÓW

Bringing your kids to Kraków is highly recommended. Children's facilities in restaurants are improving with many now offering high chairs and children's menus. Many sights cater for both small and big people, including Kazimierz's **City Engineering Museum** (see page 55), which has a hands-on section for children; **Kraków Zoo** (see page 70), with its kids' area; and the water slides at **Park Wodny** (see page 92). There is a large outdoor adventure playground in **H. Jordana Park** immediately northwest of the National Museum and an indoor playground inside **Galeria Kazimierz** (see page 92).

CALENDAR OF EVENTS

Early January New Year classical concerts deep inside the salt mines in Wieliczka (see page 72), just east of the city.

February *Sea Shanties* (www.shanties.pl): You couldn't be further from the sea but that doesn't stop this annual celebration.

March *Bach Days:* a series of concerts celebrating the music of the composer Johann Sebastian Bach.

April *Masters and Youngsters Jazz* (www.jazz.krakow.pl): Polish and international jazz; Netia *Off Camera* (https://offcamera.pl/en/): international independent film festival; PZU Cracovia Marathon (www.pzucracoviamaraton.pl).

May *Museum Night:* for one night only and lasting until the early hours, this is a fabulous, free way to enjoy the city's museums; *Photomonth in Kraków* (http://2017.photomonth.com/pl) with photographic exhibitions all over the city.

May–June *Great Dragon Parade* (www.paradasmokow.pl): in honour of the city's mythical fire-breathing dragon, including firework displays and huge flying dragons.

Early June The coronation of the king of the Kraków Marksmen Brotherhood (http://bractwo-kurkowe.pl) takes place on the Rynek.

June–July *Kraków Opera Summer Festival* (www.opera.krakow.pl): performances throughout the city, including ballet and theatre.

24 June *Wianki:* harking back to pagan days, this is a night festival of fire and feisty girls for all the family along the Wista next to Wawel.

Late June *Jewish Festival of Culture* (www.jewishfestival.pl/en/): 10 days of everything Jewish, from Yiddish language courses and Yiddish theatre to kosher cooking and live *klezmer* music, staged in various venues in Kazimierz and the Old Town.

July Ulica 26 *Street Art International Theatre Festival* (http://teatrkto.pl/): much absurdity and experimental theatre over three days in the Rynek.

August Festival of *pierogi* (traditional Polish dumplings).

September *Sausage Dog Parade:* the daft day of the dachshunds.

November–January *Christmas Market:* the Rynek stages a market, with stalls of hot soup, Christmas gifts, colourful lights and carol concerts.

EATING OUT

Luckily, the days when all visitors had to say about Polish food was that there was an awful lot of cabbage in it, are gone. The gastronomic revolution that has swept through Poland in the last decade has also reached Kraków, with new restaurants opening in the blink of an eye (and some closing down equally fast). The Poles are fanatical meat-eaters, and especially in the south, where there's a healthy Goral, or highlander, influence, they make an extremely good job of cooking it. Despite this, vegetarian dishes, gluten-free and vegan cuisine are becoming increasingly popular, even in the relatively conservative Kraków.

A classic Polish meal might be soup with plenty of white and/or rye bread to start, followed by a main course of pork or chicken accompanied by the ubiquitous potato and vegetables, which are often served raw and will almost certainly include a little salad of shredded cabbage, white or red. Meals finish with a range of desserts: the Poles excel both in preparing and consuming these.

RESTAURANTS

Kraków's restaurant scene expands like a runaway soufflé, with new and interesting places opening all the time. You'll find the greatest concentration of restaurants in the Old Town, whose wide variety of establishments offer everything from classic *pierogi* to poppadoms. The Old Town is also by far the most expensive place to eat in the city, but prices are never-theless reasonable when compared with Western Europe. Kazimierz is primarily the nerve centre of the city's drinking culture, but does also boast Jewish restaurants as well as the best Indian food in Kraków. As you venture outwards from the centre, the choices becomes less exciting, but again there are one or two exceptions to the rule.

As well as having every conceivable type of Polish cuisine, the city plays host to a plethora of international options, from kebabs to pizza (a Polish institution) to sushi. Many kitchens are now run by experienced chefs from abroad. While Poland is by no means known for vegetarian cuisine, the attitude is slowly changing. Meat-free options include Glonojad (see page 108) and Momo (see page 111).

Menus in English are available in most places, and waiting staff in all but the lowliest of city-centre restaurants speak English, and quite often German as well. Much the same as the city's bars, many restaurants set up tables and chairs outdoors during the summer.

Cafés in Rynek Glowny

WHEN TO EAT

Breakfast (śniadanie) is usually eaten between 7am and 10am. Poles, including the inhabitants of Kraków, favour a cold breakfast, typically of bread, cheese, ham and a little salad. Hot breakfast, including an omelette, is gaining popularity and will be found on all but the cheapest hotel breakfast menus. Hotel breakfasts in general are undergoing a much-needed overhaul, with cold buffets being replaced with a more international style. Tea is taken without milk.

Lunch (obiad) starts from as early as 11am and can go on until around 3pm. Business lunches are becoming more and more popular. For most Poles, dishes are basic, with a three-course meal made up of a simple soup with plenty of white or rye bread, a main course consisting of usually meat and plenty of cabbage, and a simple dessert. Alcohol is generally not drunk during lunch.

Dinner (kolacja) is eaten between 6pm and 9pm. Meals tend to be similar to those eaten at lunchtime. Poland is a nation of traditionalists, and dinnertime remains a home-based family affair. As Western standards continue to influence Polish culture, going out for dinner is becoming more popular.

MEAT, FISH AND VEGETARIAN OPTIONS

For almost all Poles a meal of substance includes meat. Pork is by far the most popular. One classic is pork cutlet, coated in breadcrumbs and served with stewed cabbage. Roast pork is eaten both hot and cold. Beef is less common, though zrazy zawijane (beef rolls filled with bacon, dark bread and mushrooms) is a standard dish. The meat dish not to be missed is bigos.

Game is very popular, as you might expect from the national affinity for meat and rich tastes. Roe deer (sarna) is usually

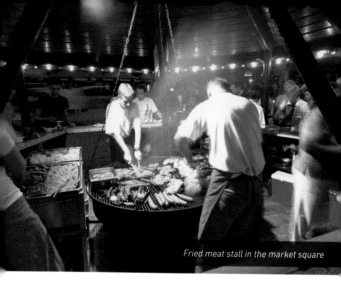

Fried meat stall in the market square

reserved for elite restaurants, as are wild boar *(dzik)* and other 'exotic' game. Look, too, for hare *(zając)* and pheasant *(bażant)*. Chicken *(kurczak)* is common and inexpensive. Polish chicken is typically stuffed and roasted. Chicken soup is a great Polish favourite, as is roasted duck *(kaczka)* with apples.

Fish is popular, with pike, eel, perch, sturgeon and others – boiled, fried or roasted – found in most good restaurants. Carp is a particular favourite (especially on Christmas Eve), often served in aspic or Polish sauce with raisins and almonds.

Vegetarians should look for potato pancakes or dumplings stuffed with fruit, *kopytka* (gnocchi), *pierogi* filled with cheese and potato, and crêpes. Salads include tomato salads, sliced cucumbers in sour cream, and coleslaw.

AN A–Z OF DISHES
You will bump into the following dishes everywhere you go.

Bigos is a simple dish of sauerkraut with onions, a variety of meat, game and/or sliced sausage and occasionally mushrooms, simmered for hours and eaten on its own (or with bread).

Gołąbki ('pigeons') are cabbage leaves stuffed with minced beef, onions and rice.

Made with anything from beef to turkey to bison, *kiełbasa* (Polish sausages) are excellent. *Krakowska* is a traditional local sausage with pepper and garlic.

The undisputed Polish folk dish is *pierogi*, small dough parcels filled with anything from minced pork or beef to cabbage or potato to sweet berries, and served with sour cream.

Placki are made by grating a potato to a pulp, mixing it with flour and egg, and then frying the result. Again, they are served with sour cream, or often goulash.

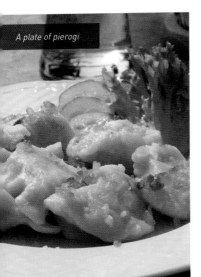

A plate of pierogi

Smalec is, in a word, lard. Traditionally with fresh bread and a beer, you might find it instead of butter in the breadbasket in a folk restaurant.

Zapiekanki are Polish pizzas. For sale in every underpass in the nation, a *zapiekanka* is essentially a sliced baguette covered with mushrooms and melted cheese, smothered with tomato ketchup, and eaten while walking.

The two most common types of *zupa* (soup) are *żurek*, a hot and, if

⊙ CAFÉ CULTURE

Kraków's café culture is, like the people who inhabit the city, richly varied. When the sun is shining, there's perhaps nothing quite as relaxing as sitting under a café umbrella and sipping on a drink. There's even something special about sitting inside a café and watching the rain fall relentlessly for hours on end as it does from time to time. The following cafés represent a mere handful of the city's multitude of outstanding establishments.

In the market square, **Słodki Wentzl** (Rynek Główny 19) serves good coffee and even better puddings, cakes and artisan ice cream, with vegan options also available. With a nice terrace for the summer, it is excellent spot for a daytime pick-me-up as well as a quiet evening beer or wine.

More typical of young Kraków is **Café Szafe** (Felicjanek 10; www.cafeszafe.com), a friendly place with quirky decor that hosts all sorts of arty evening happenings from live bands to poetry readings.

Miss the **Noworolski** (Rynek Główny 1/3; www.noworolski. com.pl), in the Cloth Hall, at your peril. This historic place is known for its plush Art Nouveau interior excellent cakes and coffee. This was Vladimir Lenin's favourite haunt during his stay in the city between 1912 and 1914.

Café Bona (ul. Kanoniczna 11) serves some of the best coffee in town, together with a good range of sandwiches, tarts and home-made cakes. It's also a bookshop with some titles available in English.

The cosy **Mleczarnia** (ul. Beera Meiselsa 20; http://mle czarnia.wroclaw.pl/krakow) is a true Kazimierz institution, with a lovely summer garden, old black-and-white photographs, tasty breakfasts and amazing coffee.

well-made, thick, sour rye soup with sausages and potatoes, and *barszcz*, a thin beetroot soup served with dumplings.

LOCAL SPECIALITIES

The *precel* (also known as an *obwarzanek*) is a fabulously doughy white bread roll in the shape of a bagel, often sprinkled with seeds including poppy and sesame. Available for about 1zł, they are sold from little barrows set up on every street corner in the city.

Originating in the Tatras, but for sale from seemingly every old lady's basket in Kraków, an *oscypek* is a spindle-shaped cheese covered in elaborate folk patterns. Made traditionally from sheep milk, *oscypki* are smoked, have a texture somewhere between a hard and soft cheese, and come in bite-sized versions as well as the classic size and occasional monster. Many stalls can be found in Zakopane selling hot *oscypek* straight from a barbecue grill, on which you'll also find the main ingredient in the local Goral food, big hunks of roast mutton from the nearby mountains.

Tip on tipping

When tipping, one thing to be aware of to avoid an embarrassing and costly situation is that thanking your waiting staff as you hand them your cash is interpreted as an invitation to trouser the change. Save all forms of plaudits until what's owed to you has been safely delivered.

SWEETS

Two things to look out for are the sublime *kremówka*, a cream cake that comes in all manner of gooey and sickly varieties, and the local Wawel chocolate, available in simple bars and fancy tins; there's even a magnificent 90 percent cocoa variety. They make excellent gifts and souvenirs. The Wawel

Oscypki (smoked sheep's cheese)

Royal Castle Shop (Wawel 9; tel: 012 422 05 90; www.wawel.com.pl; open daily 9am–5pm) is a good place to see the full range.

WHAT TO DRINK

With the microbrewery trend firmly entrenched, Polish beers are quickly catching up with their more famous brews produced by neighbours Germany, the Czech Republic and Lithuania. Among the best-known brands of Polish beer are Żywiec, Okocim, Warka, Łomża and Tyskie.

Poland does, however, claim to be the motherland of vodka which, whether true or not, doesn't stop the Poles from making some of the best vodka in the world. A baffling battalion of brands awaits the vodka virgin, of which the classiest and cleanest are Belvedere and Chopin (who never touched a drop in his life). Most ubiquitous is the excellent Wyborowa. Among the many flavoured vodkas the

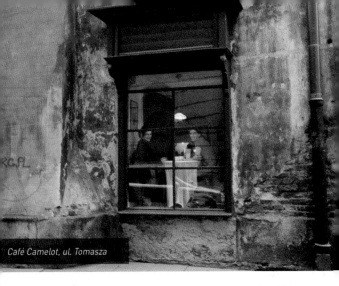

best is Żubrówka, flavoured with a single blade of bison-grass (hence the beast on the label) and with a smell and taste like that of a putting green after rain.

Less celebrated is *starka*, a dark and almost syrupy vodka made from rye grain and flavoured with lime flowers and apple leaves. Around since at least the 15th century, *starka* is aged in oak barrels and was traditionally buried in the ground for up to 50 years. This potent spirit can have an alcohol content of over 50 percent. Try the excellent Polmos brand from the town of Szczecin, the only word you'll be able to say after a few glasses of the stuff. Slightly less dangerous is the equally unpronounceable *grzaniec galicyjski*, a local concoction of heated wine flavoured with cloves.

Wine production is in its infancy in Poland and you are unlikely to see Polish names on a wine list. This may be about to change since Kraków's Jagiellonian University started its own vineyard in 2005 and the city's University of Agriculture began courses in viticulture and oenology in 2012. Imported wines are widely available. Their quality and selection have vastly improved over the recent years while prices have fallen. The cheaper choices are Hungarian and Bulgarian; more expensive are French, Italian and Spanish wines.

Coffee *(kawa)* is a favourite drink and is generally served black (unless you ask for milk) or with a just a dash of milk. Espresso and cappuccino are widely available. Tea *(herbata)*, which is usually served with lemon, is also drunk by most Poles.

TO HELP YOU ORDER...

A table for one/two/three/four people, please
Proszę stolik na jedną osobę dwie/trzy/cztery osoby
Waiter/waitress! **Proszę pana!/ Proszę pani!**
The bill, please. **Proszę rachunek**

MENU READER

barszcz beetroot soup
befsztyk beef steak
bigos sauerkraut and meat dish
chleb bread
frytki chips/fries
gołąbki stuffed cabbage leaves
golonka pork knuckle
grzyb mushroom
herbata tea
warzywa vegetables
kawa coffee
kotlet fried pork cutlet

kurczak chicken
mięso meat
ogórek cucumber
piwo beer
polędwica beef sirloin
ryba fish
ser cheese
szynka ham
woda water
wódka vodka
ziemniaki potatoes
zrazy stuffed beef rolls
zupa soup
żurek rye-flour soup

PLACES TO EAT

The following price guide refers to a three-course meal for one person, excluding drinks:

$$$$	over 200zł
$$$	100–200zł
$$	50–100zł
$	below 50zł

OLD TOWN

Not surprisingly, the Old Town features the best choice of restaurants in the city, from kebab stalls selling spicy lamb and falafel delicacies to ostentatious tourist traps with white tablecloths and Western prices. The Old Town is also the best place to try traditional Polish fare in fairytale surroundings.

Albertina Restaurant & Wine $$$-$$$$ *ul. Dominikańska 3, tel: 012 570 136 720,* http://albertinarestaurant.pl. The beautiful interior is a great setting to enjoy the creative menu of Chef Grzegorz Fic. The game, seafood and seasonal dishes are particularly good, but there are excellent vegetarian options too. The wine list is well curated, and consists of 32 labels, which have been carefully selected to complement the menu and are sold by the glass. All in all, excellent value. Open daily noon–11pm.

Aqua e Vino $$$ *ul. Wiślna 5/10, tel: 012 421 25 67,* www.aquaevino.pl. A great Italian restaurant situated in a medieval cellar with attached lounge bar, run by an Italian and thus ensuring you get both authenticity and quality. The minimalist decor includes large black-and-white photographs of famous people eating Italian food, of which the stuff served here is arguably the best in Kraków. There's a fine wine list to accompany the food too. Highly recommended. Open daily 1am–midnight.

U Babci Maliny $ *ul. Sławkowska 17, tel: 012 422 76 01,* www.kuchniaubabcimaliny.pl. A rather whimsical take on Polish food deep in the bowels of a large library, this classic family favourite, one a chain you'll find across the city, serves excellent-value *pierogi* and other traditional Polish dishes in a setting that could easily double as the set for a children's television programme. If you don't mind eating your dinner off a log amid tropical fish and other quirky trappings, you'll simply love this one. Open Mon–Fri 11am–11pm, Sat–Sun noon–11pm. Cash only. It has another branch at ul. Szpitalna 38.

Café Camelot $$ *ul. św Tomasza 17, tel: 012 421 01 23.* On a quiet corner a few steps from the Main Market Square, this popular upmarket and shaby chic café has an arty atmosphere enclosed by 13th-century stone walls. Unusually for Kraków, it is not in a cellar but at street level. Popular with university students, serves light meals, excellent salads and delicious cakes. On weekends in the basements there are performances by the Loch Camelot Theatre Group. Open daily 9am–midnight.

Chimera Salad Bar $ *ul. św. Anny 3, tel: 012 292 12 12,* http://chimera. com.pl. This buzzing cellar salad bar with a ground-floor garden for al fresco eating in summer is at the end of a passage leading off the street. Don't confuse it with the more formal U Chimera restaurant a few doors away. Choose from the salads and hot dishes at the counter with the help of friendly staff, then sit in one of the high-ceilinged vaulted rooms. High turnover ensures freshness and vegetarians and meat-eaters will both be happy here with herring salad, stuffed tomatoes and various quiches. Open daily 9am–10pm

Cyrano de Bergerac $$$ *ul. Sławkowska 26, tel: 012 411 72 88,* www.cy ranodebergerac.com.pl. Ask anyone in the tourism industry where to go for the best meal in Kraków and the chances are they'll mention this place, which represents the height of French dining in the city. The menu includes such delights as foie gras and frogs' legs alongside its excellent *pierogi*. The short but well-chosen wine list has many fine French vintages, too. Open Mon–Sun noon–11pm.

Da Pietro $$ *Rynek Główny 19, tel: 012 422 3279;* www.dapietro.pl. In business for over 25 years, this Italian eatery was one of the first privately-owned restaurants in Kraków. Located right on the Market Square, in a delightful cellar, this is a good place to get an Italian fix without breaking the bank (at least when you go for the Italian staples such as pizza or pasta). Large portions and a good list of Italian wines (sold either by the glass or by bottles). Open daily 12.30pm–midnight.

Glonojad $-$$ *Pl. Matejki 2, tel: 12 346 16 77,* www.glonojad.com. A haven for non-meat-eaters, this restaurant serves excellent vegetarian and vegan food with plenty of experimental touches. The dishes here are enormous, delicious and very cheap. Look out for the fresh salads, wonderful falafel wraps, lentil pierogis and home-made pączki (doughnuts). Friendly and knowledgeable staff add to the positive experience. Open Mon–Fri 8am–10pm, Sat–Sun 9am–10pm.

Klimaty Południa $$-$$$ *ul. Św. Gertrudy 5, tel: 012 422 03 57,* http://klimatypoludnia.pl. This small restaurant with its tranquil courtyard in summer and warm fireplace in winter, set back off the busy streets is the perfect place to eat and relax. The menu features a mix of Mediterranean and Polish cuisine. Well-curated *wine list*. Open daily 10am–midnight.

Miód Malina $$$ *ul. Grodzka 40, tel: 012 430 04 11,* http://miodmalina.pl. Cheerful restaurant with raspberries painted on the walls. Popular with tourists and tour groups, who regularly pack the place out for the purpose of eating from a fine Italian menu and sampling the fine wine list. Best to book ahead. High-quality food, nice atmosphere and reasonable prices. Open daily 10am–11pm.

Milkbar Tomasza $-$$ *ul. Św. Tomasza 24, tel: 012 422 17 06.* This stylish eatery located on one of the most picturesque streets in the city is a mix of traditional Polish bar *mleczny* ('milk bar' serving dishes based on dairy products) and American diner. The food is simple: *pierogi* (dumplings), pancakes, salads and sandwiches, but it is always fresh. Perfect for breakfasts. Friendly staff and free Wi-fi. Open Tue–Sat 8am–8pm, Sun 9am–8pm.

Moaburger $ *ul. Mikołajska 3, tel: 012 421 21 44.* This modest place is a favourite haunt of locals with a great selection of huge, tasty burgers and endless toppings. It's always busy, which vouches for the quality of the food. Open Sun–Thu 11am–11pm, Fri–Sat until midnight.

Padre $$ *ul. Wiślna 11, tel: 012 430 62 99,* http://restauracja-padre. pl. A charming terrace during the summer and a gorgeous and unpretentious cellar restaurant for the colder months, Padre serves an excellent mix of Polish and Mediterranean cuisine . The waitresses are pleasant enough and the piped music is always entertaining. Open daily 1am–10pm.

Corse $$$ *ul. Poselska 24, tel: 012 421 62 73,* www.corserestaurant. pl. Attempting to recreate a Corsican village feel in Poland is bound to miss the mark, but that's no reason to give this boat-themed restaurant a wide berth. Both the food and the service are outstanding (visiting groups should try one of the marvellous fondues), and its location, cunningly hidden in one of the Old Town's lesser-known back streets, tends to keep the hordes away. Open daily 1am–11pm.

Trzy Rybki $$$$ *ul. Szczepańska 5, tel: 012 384 08 08,* http://stary.hotel. com.pl. This smart, top-notch restaurant located on the ground floor of the Stary Hotel is arguably the best in Kraków. The high vaulted ceilings, white table cloths and impeccable service compliment the exquisite cuisine of chef Krzysztof Żurek. Excellent wines and desserts. Open daily noon–11pm.

U Romana $ *ul. Św. Tomasza 43, sixth floor, tel: 012 423 20 81 ex. 166,* http://uromana.com.pl. Cheap cafeteria located in the seat of the Kraków Music Academy. The food is simple and traditional, but the main draw here is a wonderful panoramic view over the roofs of the city. Open Mon–Fri 9am–5pm, Sun 9am–3pm.

Wentzl $$$$ *Rynek Główny 19, tel: 012 429 52 99,* http://wentzl.pl. Another venerable Kraków eating house, Wentzl has a restaurant pedigree going back to 1792, and offers a classic menu of Polish dishes enlivened by Viennese specialities. Looking at the pastel colours of its ground-floor café, you may be surprised at the ambition of the fine-dining restaurants on the first floor and in the cellar. Try the fresh foie gras. Open daily 6–11pm.

Wierzynek $$$$ *Rynek Główny 16, tel: 0728 871 171,* http://wierzynek.pl. In business since 1364, Kraków's oldest restaurant features a labyrinth of smart rooms, waitresses in 18th-century costumes, a frighteningly expensive range of regal Polish food including a good selection of game, and an illustrious guest book including such names as De Gaulle, Castro, Bush and Kate Moss. Open daily 1–11pm.

KAZIMIERZ

Kazimierz's reputation is intrinsically linked with its excellent bar and café culture. It has also a lot of good and relatively cheap dining options.

Barka $$ *Pogórska 16 (at the top of ul. Gazowej, near Kładka Bernatka), tel: 066 882 04 54.* This new kid on the Kazimierz block has created a definite stir. It is a restaurant on a Dutch barge, which offers dining on deck in summer, and a smart modern interior with a separate bar area for less fine days. The seasonal menu using traditional Polish ingredients in a refreshingly modern way, and there are vegetarian option too. Sun–Thu noon–10pm, Fri–Sun until midnight. Food is served until 9.30pm only.

Ariel $$$ *ul. Szeroka 18, tel: 012 421 79 20,* www.ariel-krakow.pl. The somewhat cluttered decor gives this restaurant the look of a curiosity shop, but if you're in town and looking for a Jewish dining experience, it's worth putting Ariel on your list. The food swerves perilously from mediocre to sublime, but the live Jewish music is always fun (every day at 8pm). Open daily 10am–midnight.

Bagelmama $ *ul. Dajwór 10B, tel: 012 346 16 46,* www.bagelmama.com. Bagelmama serves a beguiling hotchpotch of bagels and Mexican food. The chatty owner serves up delicious fresh bagels with a whole array of toppings, and there's no getting away from the fact that the bagels served here outshine those on offer in the rest of the country. Open daily 9am–5pm.

Edo $$$ *ul. Bożego Ciała 3, tel: 012 422 24 24*, www.edosushi.pl. Better than average, good-value Japanese food including great sushi in an equally fine setting. The owners boast that the only Polish ingredients used are water, sugar and salt. Although it's unlikely you're in Poland especially for the Japanese food, bear in mind that the prices make it an extremely attractive option. The private area at the back does the full no-shoes affair. Book early to avoid disappointment. Sun–Thu noon–10pm, Fri–Sat 11am–11pm.

Introligatoria Smaku $$ *ul. Józefa 20, tel: 0661 116 351*, www.introli gatorniasmaku.pl. This is another good place in Kazimierz, located in a former bookbinding workshop. The clean, modern décor gives the illusion of space to the small dining room. The menu here, featuring Polish and international staples, changes all the time. Booking essential. Open Mon–Fri from 1pm, Sat–Sun from noon until the last customers leave.

Klezmer Hois $$ *ul. Szeroka 6, tel: 012 411 12 45*, www.klezmer.pl. Housed inside the district's former Jewish bathhouse, this is fine and traditional Jewish dining at its best. The food and the surroundings make for a perfect night out, and of course there's lively Jewish music to keep the tourists happy. Of the three Jewish restaurants listed here, Klezmer Hois is most certainly the best option. Open daily 7am–9.30pm.

Momo $ *ul. Józefa Dietla 49, tel: 0609 68 57 75*, www.momotownhostel. com. Famous throughout Poland, this small and unassuming wholefood and vegetarian restaurant between the Old Town and Kazimierz provides good healthy food, from brown rice dishes to a range of excellent salads. Don't be put off by the canteen appearance – there are some truly appetising dishes on offer here, representing excellent value. Open daily 11am–8pm. Cash only.

Starka $$$ *ul. Józefa 14, tel: 012 430 65 38*, www.starka-restauracja. pl. The interior of this popular restaurant is very cosy. Think wooden beams on the ceiling, leather sofas and framed illustrations on red walls. The menu features mainly meat and fish dishes, but the wild mushroom soup is equally delicious. It's a good place to sample homemade vodkas alongside selected appetizers. Booking is essential. Open daily noon–11pm.

WEST OF THE OLD TOWN

Zielona Kuchnia $$$ *ul. Grabowskiego 8/9, tel: 012 634 55 22,* http://zielonakuchnia.eu. This place claims to serve the healthiest food based on organic and natural products and the dishes are beautifully presented. The smoked duck is really worth a try, as are the steaks and it would be a shame to miss out on the desserts. In summer, the outdoor area is heavenly. Open Mon 4–10pm, Tue–Sat from 1–10pm or last customer, Sun 1–10pm. .

EAST OF THE OLD TOWN

Bal $–$$ *Ul. Ślusarska 9, tel: 0 734 411 733.* A self-service cafeteria located conveniently near the museum of contemporary art, MOCAK, with a long table in the middle and smaller tables dotted around it. The menu changes constantly and there are also breakfast buffets. Open daily Mon 8am–9pm, Tue, Thu and Fri 8am–10pm, Wed and Sat 9am–10pm, Sun 9am–9pm.

NOWA HUTA

Following the recent push to attract coachloads of tourists to Nowa Huta, tourist authorities hope that a few decent places to eat will follow in their wake. However, the district remains sadly lacking in anything really worth sticking around for, and the following have been included more as curiosities rather than anything to write home about.

Santorini $$$ *ul. Bulwarowa 35b, tel: 012 680 51 95.* Inside the hotel of the same name (see page 140), this is Nowa Huta's first foray into the world of white tablecloths and immaculate-looking waiters. It provides an interesting mix of local and international dishes. The simple daily specials are good value. Open daily 10am–10pm.

TARNÓW

As one would expect for a provincial Polish town such as Tarnów, the quality of available dining establishments is somewhat limited. Still, it's hungry work tramping the streets, and if you choose to spend the night here you'll almost certainly need to eat something.

Restauracja Pół na Pół $-$$ *pl. Kazimierza Wielkiego 2, tel: 014 627 82 78*, http://polnapol-tarnow.pl. Handily placed in the centre of town, this restaurant and coffee shop, spread over two floors, has a well-priced creative menu featuring a choice of sandwiches with homemade bread and pasta. Lunch menu (22zł) changes weekly. A good choice for a break from sightseeing. Open Mon-Tue noon-8pm, Wed noon-11pm, Thu and Sun until 10pm, Fri-Sat until midnight.

Tarnovia $-$$ *ul. Kościuszki 10, tel: 014 630 03 50.* Situated on the ground floor of the hotel of the same name (see page 141), this elegant, white napkin restaurant has been recently renovated. The menu is an interesting mix of traditional Polish and international cuisine; the food is surprisingly good, and there are vegetarian options. Open Mon-Fri 6.30am-10pm, Sat-Sun 7am-10pm.

ZAKOPANE

The natural home of traditional, fatty, meat-heavy Goral or highlander food, Zakopane has numerous restaurants and outdoor grills serving delicious meat dishes. You'll never go hungry in this town. Many restaurants have a folksy decor, which adds greatly to the atmosphere.

Bąkowo Zohylina Niznio $$ *ul. Piłsudskiego 6, tel: 018 206 62 16,* www.niznio.zohylina.pl. This place serves what's arguably the best local cuisine in town. The meat-heavy menu includes chicken, some excellent shashlik, a lot of pork dishes and loin. It's all cooked to perfection, and for once the service hits the mark. The restaurant's rustic setting comes complete with some fine examples of folk art on the walls. It's so popular that another branch has opened in the same street at 28a (tel: 018 201 20 45; http://wyznio.pl). Open daily 1pm-midnight.

Casa Mia $$$ *ul. Krupówki 69, tel: 0 516 645 313*. This smart place on the main pedestrian street of Zakopane offers a relief for those who are tired of heavy, regional cuisine. The seasonal menu includes dishes such as salmon and beef carpaccio, and tiger prawns, as well as some French and Italian dishes. Refined versions of staples of Polish cuisine are available, too. Open daily noon–10pm. Only children over six years old are allowed to enter.

Gazdowo Kuźnia $$ *ul. Krupówki 1, tel: 018 201 72 01*, www.gazdowok-uznia.pl. Sit in a traditional wooden sleigh and eat vast plates of greasy meat dishes while being served by waitresses dressed as Heidi. If you're in town during the summer, take advantage of the restaurant's outdoor kebab stall, which sells possibly the best kebabs in Europe. The meat is cut straight from a rotating pig on a spit and served in hot, crispy white bread with heaps of salad and spicy mayonnaise. Open daily 11am–11pm.

Marzanna $ *ul. Oswalda Balzera 17e, tel: 018 206 24 61.*. This typical regional restaurant serves hearty portions making it a great option for a lunch. The menu features staples from the Zakopane region. Open daily noon–10pm, Fri until 11pm.

A–Z TRAVEL TIPS

A SUMMARY OF PRACTICAL INFORMATION

A

ACCOMMODATION (see also Youth Hostels, and the list of Recommended Hotels on page 137)

As Poland's most popular tourist destination, Kraków has ample accommodation of every standard imaginable. From very basic rooms to five-star masterpieces, Kraków's got it all. There are hotels, apartments, pensions and hostels to suit every taste, and deciding on where to stay should be based on your needs rather than your budget as prices are still below those in Western Europe. If you are in need of some peace and quiet, you should exercise caution when booking a hotel in the Old Town, which is full of bars and clubs and can be very noisy at night.

Breakfast is almost always included in the price of a room, although the meal provided varies hugely from rolls and coffee to a buffet which will keep you going all day. The official city website www.krakow-info.com/, www.staypoland.com and www.inyourpocket.com are excellent sources for finding and securing exactly the kind of accommodation you're looking for.

> I'd like a... **Chciałbym** h-tch'ahw-bim
> single **pojedynczy** po-yedinchi
> double room **podwójny pokój** po-dvooyni pokooy
> with a bath **z wanną** s van-nom
> with a shower **z prysznicem** s prishn'ee-tsem

AIRPORT (see also Getting There)

Kraków's **John Paul II International** (Balice) Airport (KRK, ul. Kapitana Medweckiego 1; tel: 012 295 58 00; www.krakowairport.pl), 18km (11 miles) west of the city, is compact and user-friendly. It is connected to the city centre by train, with departures every 30 minutes and a journey time of just 18 minutes. There is also a multi-storey car park near T1, with a cheaper long-stay car park a little farther away.

Getting to the city. The fastest option is to take the train, while alternative options include taxi or bus. Head outside where you'll find plenty of official Kraków Airport taxis (tel: 012 258 0 258, call centre operates daily from 6am to 10pm; alternatively you may a book taxi online at http://mplservices.pl/en/taxi/#taxi_rezerwacje). Make sure the meter is running and expect to pay about 70–80zł. Alternatively, outside the main airport doors is a frequent public bus service (buses 208, 252 and nightly 902) that takes you to the city centre in 40 minutes. Tickets cost 4zł and can be bought in kiosks and from ticket machines at the airport. The service runs regularly every day from around 5am until 10.30pm. There is an information desk and branch of the Kraków tourist information service inside the main terminal building.

B

BICYCLE HIRE

The mass of tourists clogging up the Old Town and the combination of trams and unpredictable drivers around the city centre makes riding a bicycle anywhere but in a park a brave undertaking. The Wavelo Bike (tel: 012 290 33 33; https://en.wavelo.pl/) emulates short-hire cycling schemes in London and Paris. To rent one, register online and then enter your 6-digit account number and 4-digit PIN into the keypad on the back of the bike to unlock it. After finishing the ride, lock your bike to Wavelo docking station. The monthly fee of 19zł allows you to ride for free for 60 minutes every day; for other fares, check the website. Biking in the city centre might not be to everyone's taste though, so an alternative is to head outside the city. Cycling from the Old Town to Tyniec Abbey should not take more than an hour and a half each way. The starting point is from Bernardynska street at the foot of Wawel: cross the river via Grunwaldzki bridge, follow ul. Tyniecka down to the river embankment and head south to Tyniec. Another good idea for a bike trip is the short excursion from Wawel to the Pilsudski Mound in the Las Wolski forest. For more information see www.krakow-info.com.

Several other companies offer bicycles for longer-term hire, of which the Kazimierz-based company Two Wheels (ul. Józefa 5; tel: 012 421 57 85; www.dwakola.internetdsl.pl; daily 10am–6pm) is arguably the best, hiring bikes for around 50zł/24 hours. Take your passport or driver's licence, leave a 100zł deposit and away you go.

BUDGETING FOR YOUR TRIP

Getting to and sleeping in Kraków are generally the two biggest expenses of a trip to the city. Once these are paid for you'll find that even by Polish standards Kraków is a relatively cheap destination. To work out the mysteries of the Polish *złoty*, see page 128.

Travel to Kraków. Flying to Kraków has never been cheaper. Budget airlines serving Kraków from the UK include easyJet (from London Gatwick, Belfast, Bristol, Liverpool Manchester, and Edinburgh; www.easyjet.com), Jet2.com (Newcastle, Manchester) and Ryanair (from Dublin, London Stansted, Liverpool, Birmingham and East Midlands; www.ryanair.com). At the top of the scale, late bookings from Heathrow with the Polish national carrier LOT (www.lot.pl) and British Airways (www.britishairways.com) can cost much more. Kraków is a 40-minute hop from Warsaw, so it's also worth looking into flying to Kraków via the capital as this route can turn up the occasional bargain. There are also many connections from Frankfurt to Kraków for those flying from North America.

Taxis. At the time of writing licensed taxis cost 7zł plus 2.30–7zł per kilometre after that, depending on the time of night.

Meals and entertainment. Eating out in Kraków runs from the ridiculously cheap to sophisticated restaurants that could give any in Europe a run for their money and price their dishes similarly. Local beer starts at about 8zł for half a litre; beer bought at hotel bars and Guinness in general is more expensive, in some cases costing as much as in the West. Cinema and theatre tickets remain very affordable, costing about 25zł for a ticket.

Museums and attractions. Almost all museums in the city open their doors once a week for free. For comprehensive cultural listings get the free Karnet magazine (www.karnet.krakow.pl) from any Kraków tourist information office and many other places around town. Entry to museums will cost about 10zł, although a set of tickets for all the sights on Wawel Hill will set you back almost 100zł, for what would be a very full day's sightseeing.

C

CAR HIRE (see also Driving)

Kraków's compact size makes hiring a car more trouble than it's worth. However, for visiting other destinations, hiring a car can be a smart move. Bear in mind that some of the Polish roads are in need of repair, and few motorways exist.

Arrangements and conditions for car hire are similar to those in other countries. The minimum age requirement is 21, and you must have been in possession of a licence valid for at least one year. Drivers from outside the EU should have an international driving licence. Ask if collision damage waiver insurance is included in the price. Prices range from around 100zł a day, and usually include unlimited mileage.

The following companies all have websites in English; Avis, Budget and Sixt have offices at the airport:

Avis: ul. Lubicz 23; tel: 012 629 61 08; www.avis.pl (also airport).

Budget: ul. Medweckiego 1 (airport) also Lubicz 23; tel: +48 601 354 669; www.budget.pl.

Krakrent: ul. Kamieńskiego 41; tel: +48 606 500 200; http://krakrent.pl/.

Europcar: ul. Nadwiślańska 6 (Qubus Hotel); tel: +48 665 301 617; www.

I'd like to hire a car. **Chcę wynająć samochód** h-tseh vinayontch' samohoot

I'd like it for a day a week **Chcę na dzień/tydzień** h-tseh na djyeng'/tidjyeng'

What's the charge per day/week? **Ile kosztuje jeden dzień/tydzień?** eeleh koshtooyeh jedendjyeng'/tidjyeng'

europcar.com.pl.
Hertz: al. Focha 1, also airport; tel: 012 429 62 62; www.hertz.com.pl.
Joka: ul. Zacisze 7; tel: 0601 54 53 68; www.joka.com.pl.
Sixt: ul. Kapitana Medweckiego 1 (airport), also train station; tel: +48 661 999 175; www.sixt.pl.

CLIMATE

Kraków is somewhat warmer than most Polish cities, although its temperate climate guarantees little more than warmish summers with random downpours of rain. The city generally gets a week or two of blisteringly hot sunshine, but it's impossible to predict when this will happen. Spring and autumn are long, and punctuated by endless overcast days. Winter isn't as predictable as it once was. The long, snowy seasons of the past are becoming less common. In winter the air quality can be quite poor, with large parts of the city cloaked in smog due to the fact that thousands of people still use coal fires as a means of heating.

	J	F	M	A	M	J	J	A	S	O	N	D
min °C	-5	-5	-1	3	9	12	15	14	10	5	1	-2
max °C	0	1	7	13	20	22	24	23	19	14	6	3
min °F	23	23	30	37	48	54	59	57	50	41	34	28
max °F	32	34	45	55	68	72	75	73	66	57	43	37

CLOTHING

While you will pack according to the season, remember that Polish clouds are fickle. As well as protection against the rain, bring comfortable footwear that can cope with Kraków's cobblestones. Beware the big temperature drop that can chill the bones after the sun sets during all but the hottest of summer days. Be prepared, and carry a light jacket or sweater.

There are one or two cultural differences worth noting that might affect what you choose to wear on certain occasions. The Poles like to dress up whenever they can. This means that turning up for the theatre, opera or at a fancy restaurant in anything but a suit or evening dress can be embarrassing.

When entering a Catholic church it's considered respectful for men to take off their hats and to keep their legs and, if possible, arms covered. Similarly, women should cover their shoulders and upper arms in church. Men should cover their heads when entering a synagogue. *Yarmulkes* (skullcaps) are usually provided for visitors.

CONSULATES

UK ul. Sw. Anny 9, tel: 012 422 42 64 (honorary consulate).

US ul.Stolarska 9; tel: 012 424 51 00; www.usembassy.gov/poland/.

Embassies (in Warsaw)

UK ul. Kawalerii 12, tel: 22 311 00 00; www.gov.uk/world/organisations/british-embassy-warsaw

Australia ul. Nowogrodzka 11; tel: 022 521 34 44; http://poland.embassy.gov.au.

Canada ul. Jana Matejki 1/5; tel: 022 584 31 00; www.canadainternational.gc.ca/poland-pologne/contact-contactez.aspx.

Republic of Ireland ul. Mysia 5; tel: 022 564 22 00; www.dfa.ie/irish-embassy/poland/.

South Africa ul. Koszykowa 54; tel: 022 622 10 31; www.dirco.gov.za/warsaw.

CRIME AND SAFETY (see also Police)

Kraków poses no real threats beyond the occasional petty thief. Don't leave valuables in plain view and take extra care in any crowded space. As in any city of this size, exercise caution when walking around late at night.

D

DISABLED TRAVELLERS

All new buildings and building renovation work in Poland must meet rigid

EU standards concerning the provision of facilities for the disabled. Places in Kraków such as the airport, many hotels and quite a few restaurants are now up to good European standards, despite the difficulty of reconciling the preservation of the Unesco-listed heritage of a medieval city with the needs of wheelchair users. Though more recently opened hotels such as the Stary have shown the way by providing wheelchair facilities in 14th-century buildings, Kraków's cobbled streets and many of its best sights remain hard work for wheelchair users and travellers with other disabilities. Wheelchair users can get around the city fairly easily on most forms of public transport. All new 'bendy' buses are designed for wheelchairs, as are the modern trams (for latest information see: www.mpk.krakow.pl).

DRIVING (see also Car Hire)

It's sobering that Polish traffic fatality figures are among the worst in Europe, mainly a testament to the unsafe driving practices of the locals. Poles drive on the right-hand side of the road unless overtaking, which is often done on narrow roads, around bends, and when approaching the brow of a hill.

For those who insist on driving in Kraków, be warned that road works are everywhere. If you are following a tram in Kraków on a road that doesn't have a separate, fenced-off area for them, proceed with caution. You are expected to stop when trams do, regardless of what lane you're in, as people will be getting on and off.

The stretch of the A4 between Katowice and Kraków is a toll road. Car drivers must pay 20zł when both joining and leaving it.

Rules and regulations. You can drive in Poland on an EU or US licence. Dipped headlights must be switched on at all times year round; seat belts are compulsory front and back and the maximum blood-alcohol limit is effectively zero.

Speed limits. 140km/h (87mph) on motorways, 120km/h (75mph) on dual carriageways, 100km/h (60mph) on single carriageways, 90km/h (55mph) outside urban areas, and 50km/h (30mph) in built-up areas. You may be fined on the spot for speeding.

Breakdowns. If you need roadside assistance, dial 022 96 37. The National Roadside Assistance Service aims to arrive within 60 minutes. The fee depends on the type of repair required and the towing distance. Car hire firms often make their own arrangements. If you are driving from your home country, your own national motoring organisation may have its own breakdown cover scheme.

car **auto/samochód**
petrol station **stacja benzynowa**
petrol/gas **benzyna**
unleaded fuel **benzyna bezołowiowa**
parking **parking**
detour **objazd**
stop **stop**
one-way street **ulica jednokierunkowa**
no passing **nie wyprzedzać**

E

ELECTRICITY

All electricity in Poland is 220v AC, 50 Hz. Sockets are the standard round, two-pin European variety with a protruding earth pin. Travellers from outside continental Europe need to bring an adaptor and those from North America will also need a transformer.

EMERGENCIES (see also Police)

The telephone numbers of the three main emergency services are listed below.

Ambulance: **999**

Fire: **998**

Police: **997**

General emergency number from mobile phones: **112**
English speakers can call a separate line for foreigners: 0 608 599 999/022 278 77 77

> I want to report an accident **Chcę zgłosić wypadek** h-tseh z-gwosh'eetch' **vipadek**
> Call a doctor! **Wezwijcie lekarza!** vez-veey-tch'yeh lekazha
> Fire! **Pali się!** palee sh'yeh

G

GAY AND LESBIAN TRAVELLERS

Catholic Poland is a largely conservative country when it comes to social mores. That said, in 2011 Kraków elected Europe's first transgendered member of parliament.

Excellent gay-friendly accommodation is listed on page 139, and though gay clubs are not numerous, there are some popular ones (https://rainbow-europe.org/) (see page 88). A handy gay guide to the city can be found by following the Kraków links at www.inyourpocket.com and www.local-life.com/krakow. The age of consent in Poland is 15.

GETTING THERE (see also Airport)

Low-cost flights have wiped out the need for a long international bus ride to Kraków. Trains remain popular, but are expensive.

By air. Serving over 5 million passengers a year, Kraków's John Paul II International Airport is the second-busiest airport in Poland after Warsaw. It offers direct flights to many European destinations, while Polish destinations include Gdańsk, and Warsaw (from where you can fly to a number of other Polish cities). Flight time from London is just over two hours. The budget airline business is in constant flux. Prices vary enormously according to many factors including airport taxes at departure, the price of aviation fuel, special promotions and how far ahead you book.

Airlines, many of which are budget carriers, flying in and out of the city include Austrian Airlines, British Airways, Brussels Airlines, easyJet, Eurowings, Germanwings, Jet2.com, KLM, LOT, Lufthansa, Norwegian, Swiss, Vueling and, Ryanair.

By rail. International trains arrive in Kraków from Berlin, Budapest, Prague and Vienna.

There are various train routes you can take between London and Kraków, involving as many as six or as few as two changes. One of the quickest involves changing in Paris and then Berlin and takes a little less than 24 hours; though the route via Brussels, Cologne and Warsaw is faster; it involves more changes. Both International Rail (www.international rail.com; tel 044 (0) 871 231 0790) and Deutsche Bahn (www. bahn.com; tel: 08718 80 80 66) book train journeys across Europe. For more information about rail journeys across Europe, visit www.seat61. com. Kraków's main railway station (Dworzec Główny) is five minutes' walk northeast of the Old Town. ATMs are in the main building if you need cash. All trains to Tarnów and Zakopane leave from this station.

The poor but hardy may want to make the trip by coach: Eurolines has thrice-weekly departures from London Victoria changing in Berlin. The whole trip takes about 27hrs 30mins and costs from €135 return.

GUIDES AND TOURS

Knowing where to go and who to go with can be confusing. Almost every hotel in Kraków offers at least one tour and will give you advice on what to see. The official Kraków tourist information offices listed on page 133 will give advice on tours, and all have stacks of brochures offering a wide range of trips, ranging from Jewish walking tours of Kazimierz to outings to Wieliczka and Auschwitz. For more tours try:

Free. Try out some different themed walking tours around Kraków in English for free, including Old Kraków, Jewish Kraków, Food and Street

Art. http://freewalkingtour.com.

Communist. Take a guided tour of Nowa Huta in an old Trabant with Crazy Guides; www.crazyguides.com.

Papal. Ride the yellow multimedia Papal Train to Pope John Paul II's birthplace in nearby Wadowice; www.pociag-papieski.pl.

H

HEALTH AND MEDICAL CARE

Visiting Poland poses no great health risks. The tap water is perfectly safe to drink but it doesn't taste as good as bottled water. UK and EU citizens with a valid European Health Insurance Card (EHIC; available from post offices or online at www.ehic.org.uk in the UK) can receive reduced-cost or even free treatment, although private medical insurance is still recommended. Whereas the difference between private and public healthcare in the West is generally a question of waiting time, state healthcare in Poland is of a much lower standard than its private cousin. An English-speaking medical emergency and ambulance telephone service (Medicina; tel: 012 266 96 65/417 35 44) is available 24 hours a day.

24-hour chemist. Apteka, ul. Galla 26, tel: 012 636 73 65.

Where's the nearest pharmacy? **Gdzie jest najbliższa apteka?** g-djyeh yest nay-bleesh-sha apteka

L

LANGUAGE

Polish, along with Czech, Slovakian and Serbian, is one of the western Slavic languages, and is written using Latin letters with the occasional diacritic thrown in to confuse non-speakers. The Poles excel in running consonants together in such a way as to terrify all but the hardiest of polyglots. The good news is that the majority of people working in the tourist industry in Kraków speak good English and/or German. Attempting a few basic words is always a nice thing to do and is appreciated by the locals. As a general rule, the accent falls on the penultimate syllable.

yes **tak** tak
no **nie** n'yeh
please **proszę** prrosheh
thank you **dziękuję** djyen'kooyeh
hi **cześć** chesh'tch'
good morning **dzień dobry** djyen' dobrri
good afternoon **dzień dobry** djyen' dobrri
good evening **dobry wieczór** dobrri v-yechoorr
good-bye **do widzenia** do vee-dzen'ya
Excuse me!/Sorry! **Przepraszam!** pshe-prrasham
Do you speak English? **Czy mówi pan/pani po angielsku?**
    chi moovee pan/panee po an-g-yelskoo
I understand. **Rozumiem.** rro-zoom-yem
I don't understand. **Nie rozumiem.** n'yeh rro-zoom-yem
My name is... **Nazywam się** nazivam sh'yeh
When? **Kiedy?** kyedi
Where is it? **Gdzie jest?** g-djyeh yest
on the left **na lewo** na levo
on the right **na prawo** na prravo
open **otwarty** ot-farrti
closed **zamknięty** zam-k-n'yenti
old/new **stary/nowy** starri/ novi
and/or **i/albo** ee/albo
also/but **również/ale** rroov-n'yesh/a-leh

M

MAPS

Free maps can be picked up in tourist information centres, hotels, bars, restaurants and cafés. A good option is the Compass 1:15,000 scale map of Kraków (about 5zł), which covers the city in detail, lists public transport routes and has the only decent map of Nowa Huta in print. You can find it in the Empik bookshop listed below.

MEDIA

International newspapers and magazines can be found in better hotels. The Empik bookshop (Rynek Główny 23; tel: 022 451 40 20; Mon–Fri 9am–8pm, Sat–Sun 11am–11pm) also stocks a small selection of foreign press, as well as maps. The monthly, English-language *Kraków Post* newspaper (www.krakowpost.com) carries news about the city and the country and is widely available. A fine monthly events magazine, *Karnet*, is available free in kiosks and hotels (http://karnet.krakow.pl/).

Many of the televisions in the better hotels in the city come with BBC World and CNN as standard. A couple of sports bars that show Premiership football etc. are listed on page 86 .

MONEY

The Polish złoty (zł) is made up of 100 groszy. At the time of writing, 1zł was worth about £0.21 (there are about 4.88zł to £1). ATMs can be found all over Kraków and are the most convenient and eco-

I want to change some dollars/pounds **Chciałbym wymienić dolary/funty** h-tch'ahw-bim vim-yenitch' dolarri/foonti

What's the exchange rate? **Jaki jest kurs waluty?** yakee yest koors valooti nomical way of obtaining Polish cash. Currency exchanges (*kantor*) are abundant and credit cards are accepted in most places. In Nowa Huta, Tarnów and Zakopane the cash payment is more usual; carry some on you at all times. Traveller's cheques can be exchanged only in a few places: bank Pekao S.A. (Rynek Główny 31), Currency Express (Floriańska 53) and the Małopolskie Centrum Informacji Turystycznej (Grodzka 31/7).

O

OPENING TIMES

Banks. Banks open early, usually at 8/9am and stay open until around 5/6pm. Most banks are closed over the weekend.

Shops. Most shops open at either 9am or 10am, stay open until about 6pm, work shorter hours on Saturdays. In 2018, a trade ban was introduced. Consequently, nearly all trading is suspended on at least two Sundays each month; by 2020 the ban is set to cover every Sunday.

Bars and restaurants. Cafés open at about 8am, while bars can open at any time between 10am and 10pm and stay open well into the night – or 'until the last guest' as they are fond of declaring. For restaurant opening times see page 106.

Museums and galleries. These generally open at 10am, and close at any time from 2pm to 6pm. Most museums don't open on a Monday.

Where's the nearest police station? **Gdzie jest najbliższy komisariat?** g-djyeh yest nuy-bleesh-shi komeesarr-yat
My ... has been stolen from my car **Ukradli mi ... z mojego samochodu** ookrrad-lee mee ... z moyego samo-hodoo
wallet **portfel** porrt-fel
handbag **torebkę** torrep-keh
passport **passport** pashporrt

P

POLICE (see also Crime and Safety and Emergencies)

You'll often spot police on the beat in the Old Town, where there's a police station *(posterunek policji)* at Rynek Główny 29 (tel: 012 615 73 17) which never closes. City guards (tel: 986 or 012 411 00 45) also patrol the Old Town. Of the many other police stations in the city, you might find the one in Kazimierz (ul. Szeroka 35; tel: 012 615 29 14) the handiest.

POST OFFICES

Kraków's main post office (Poczta Główna) is just east of the Old Town on the corner of ul. Wielopole at ul. Westerplatte 20 (tel: 012 422-24-97; Mon–Fri 8am–8.30pm, Sat 8am–3pm). A baffling queue ticket system is in operation, although stamps can be bought without queuing at windows 2–14. You can also buy stamps at newsagents and kiosks, bookshops selling postcards and tourist information centres. There's a small post office inside Wawel's main ticket office (daily 9am–4pm), which is never busy and has English-speaking staff, but does not accept parcels. Postboxes around the city are red with a yellow post horn set against a blue oval.

A stamp for this postcard/letter please **Proszę znaczek na tę pocztówkę/list** prrosheh z-nacheck na teh poch-toofkeh leest
airmail **lotniczą** lotn'eechom
registered **pocztą poleconą** pochtom poletso-nom

PUBLIC HOLIDAYS

1 January New Year's Day
6 January Epiphany

March/April Easter Sunday and Easter Monday
1 May Labour Day
3 May Constitution Day
May/June Pentecost (7th Sunday after Easter)
June Corpus Christi (9th Thursday after Easter)
15 August Feast of the Assumption
1 November All Saints' Day
11 November Independence Day
25 December First Christmas Day
26 December Second Christmas Day

R

RELIGION

The Poles have been proud Catholics for over a thousand years, a fact borne out by the Vatican's decision in 1978 to elect the first non-Italian pontiff in 455 years. Pope John Paul II rose through the ranks in Kraków and returned to the city more than once. He's considered by the nation as one of the main driving forces behind the collapse of Communism. His image can be found everywhere, and he remains an enormous focus of pride for the country.

T

TELEPHONES

Public telephones. The combined internet and mobile phone revolution has all but seen the death of public telephones in Poland. If you can actually find one, a Kraków public telephone is either yellow or silver and works using prepaid cards bought from any shop or kiosk selling sweets and cigarettes.

Mobile phones. Travellers from US and other non-EU countries can avoid roaming costs by putting a local prepaid SIM card in your mobile phone. Several companies now offer ridiculously cheap start-up packages for less than 10zł, with top-up cards costing 10zł and upwards. Both can be bought from shops and kiosks around the city as well as the airport, bus and railway stations and the Empik bookshop (see page 128). *Roaming charges were scrapped in the EU on 15 June 2017.*

Making the call. To call Kraków from outside the country, dial your international access code followed by 48 for Poland and the subscriber number minus the initial 0. The 012 at the start of a Kraków number is both part of the number and the code for the city. If you're calling Kraków from anywhere in Poland, including Kraków on a landline or from a Polish mobile you simply dial the 9-digit number. To get a line out of Poland, dial 00 plus the country code.

> telephone card **karta telefoniczna** karrteh tele-foneech-nom

TIME DIFFERENCES

Poland is on Central European Time (CET), which is one hour ahead of GMT. As in the rest of Europe, the clocks go forward one hour on the last Sunday of March and back again on the last Sunday of October.

New York	London	**Kraków**	Jo'burg	Sydney	Auckland
6am	11am	**noon**	1pm	10pm	midnight

TIPPING

As Poland becomes increasingly Westernised, tipping is slowly taking over from what went before it, namely a gracious compliment on the quality of the service performed and no more. Tipping is now firmly established in the Old Town and much of Kazimierz, the usual sum being

10 percent or a rounding up of the bill, but it's still rare in the suburbs as well as in Tarnów and Zakopane. (See page 102).

TOILETS

Toilets are marked with a triangle on the door for men and a circle for women. Do not try to use a public toilet in a restaurant or café where you're not a customer. Some places, such as McDonald's on Rynek Główny, charge 1zł or more to use their facilities, whether you are a customer or not. However there are several clean public toilets dotted around the Planty. The shopping malls listed on page 91 have free toilet facilities.

men's toilet **męski (panowie)**
women's toilet **damski (panie)**

TOURIST INFORMATION

The official Kraków City Tourist Office has several branches throughout the city (www.infokrakow.pl). The main offices are located at the following addresses:

Cloth Hall, Main Market Square 1–3; daily 9am–7pm; tel: 012 16.

Wyspiański Pavillion, pl. Wszystkich Świętych 2; daily 9am–5pm; tel: 012 354 27 23.

ul. Szpitalna 25; daily 9am–7pm; tel: 012 354 27 20.

ul. św. Jana 2; daily 9am–7pm; tel: 012 354 27 25.

ul. Powiśle 11; daily 9am–5pm; tel: 012 417 58 10.

ul. Józefa 7 (Kazimierz); daily 9am–5pm; tel: 012 354 27 28.

International Airport Kraków International Airport – Balice; daily 9am–7pm; tel: 012 285 53 41.

The Tourist Information Call Centre is open daily 9am–5pm; tel: 012 432 00 60.

Małopolska Region Tourist Information Office Rynek Główny 1–3 (within the Cloth Hall); daily 9am–7pm,; tel: 012 421 77 06; www.mcit.pl. This great little tourist information centre is the best place if you're looking to explore outside the city. It's an essential stop for anyone wanting to get the most out of a trip to Tarnów or Zakopane.

The Jewish Cultural Information Office (Centrum Kultury Żydowskiej, ul. Meiselsa 17, Kazimierz; Mon–Fri 10am–6pm, Sat–Sun 10am–2pm; tel: 012 430 64 49; www.judaica.pl) has information on Jewish cultural events.

For general information before you leave home, contact the Polish National Tourist Office:

UK: Polish National Tourist Office, Westgate House, West Gate, London W5 1YY; tel: 0300 303 1812; **US:** Polish National Tourist Office, 5 Marine View Plaza, Hoboken, New Jersey, NJ 07030; tel: 201 420 99 10.

TRANSPORT

Public transport in Kraków is both cheap and reliable. The fabulous tram system provides the perfect way of getting around, from 5am to 11pm. Tram tickets cost 3.80zł per ride on one tram over any distance. Better value are 24-hour, 48-hour and 72-hour tickets, costing 15zł, 24zł and 36zł respectively. Buy them from most kiosks or anywhere you see a 'Sprzedaż Biletów MPK' sign. Tickets must be validated in one of the yellow machines on boarding. People travelling on a single 3.80zł ticket who are in possession of an item bigger than 20 x 40 x 60cm (8 x 16 x 24in), eg a large suitcase, need to buy a ticket for that as well. Be careful when getting off trams in the city centre, where they share the roads with cars. You're essentially stepping down into traffic.

Taxis. If you want to stay the right side of bankrupt, the golden rule is: when you want a taxi, always choose licensed, metered ones. These are easily

I'd like a ticket to ... please. **Proszę o bilet do...**prrosheh o beelet do
single (one-way) **w jedną stronę** v yed-nom strroneh
return (round trip) **powrotny** povvrotni

recognisable by a large light on the roof displaying the company's name and telephone number. A sticker on the back window will show current prices. **Barbakan**, tel: 196 61 (http://barbakan.krakow.pl/). **Mega**, tel: 012 196 25 (http://megataxi.pl/). **Radio Taxi 919**, tel: 012 191 91 (https://radio taxi919.pl/en/).

V

VISAS AND ENTRY REQUIREMENTS

Holders of European Union passports do not need a visa to enter Poland and may stay as long as they please, though those staying longer than three months must register at Małopolski Urząd Wojewódzki (ul. Basztowa 22), where all visa matters are dealt with. Visitors holding passports from many other countries, such as the US, Canada and Australia, may also enter Poland without a visa but their stay may be limited, usually for 90 days. Poland is a member of the Schengen group of countries, meaning that a Schengen Block visa is valid for entry to Poland. Travellers may need to fulfil additional medical, insurance and financial requirements to be granted a visa. Visa applications need to be registered online at https://secure.e-konsulat.gov.pl/, where there is more detailed visa information. Minimum visa processing times range from 10 days to a month, depending on the passport held, and can take longer.

W

WEBSITES AND INTERNET ACCESS

http://krakow.travel/en/ The official Kraków tourist information website.
www.cracowonline.com Lists most events in the city, ranging from exhibitions to Dada theatre.
www.visitmalopolska.pl Another good source of information about the region and its capital Kraków.
www.krakow4u.pl An enthusiast's site for those interested in churches and old buildings, has detailed information and wonderful images.

Internet access. Travellers can access free wi-fi on their laptops and smartphones in and around the Main Market Square (Rynek Główny) in the Old Town (ul. Grodzka, Pl. Wszystkich Świętych, Barbakan, Pl. Matejki) and in ul. Szeroka in Kazimierz. Look out, too, for the hotspot Cracovia logo signalling free wi-fi at hotels and cafés.

Y

YOUTH HOSTELS

With more than 60 hostels in the city, ranging from spartan shoeboxes to city-centre party hostels, making the right decision about where to stay can be daunting. All of the following hostels are suitable for every kind of budget traveller regardless of age or lifestyle preference. Keep in mind that hotel prices in Kraków are lower than in most Western countries, so hostels are only really worth considering if you're on the very tightest of budgets – and the best get booked up far in advance.

Mundo Hostel ul. Józefa Sarego 10, tel: 012 422 61 13; http://en.mundohostel.eu/. Conveniently located between the Old Town and Kazimierz, this hostel offers comfortable rooms (twin and double) as well as beds in four and six-people dorms (60zł per person).

Hostel Rynek 7 Rynek Główny 7/6; tel: 012 431 16 98; www.hostel-rynek7.pl. The dormitories here look out onto the Rynek and Cloth Hall; the twin rooms are at the back of the building. This is a pleasant and re-laxed place, with good security and the opportunity to fall into bed from any one of hundreds of bars and clubs within easy walking distance.

Pink Panther's ul. Św. Tomasz 8; tel: 012 422 09 35; http://pinkpanthershostel.com It provides a good base at a good price and little else. It's more peaceful than many, and the Old Town location is one of the best there is.

Secret Garden Hostel ul. Skawińska 7; tel: 012 430 54 45; www.thesecretgarden.pl. Located in old Kazimierz, this hotel offers two different standards of rooms: economy (with shared bathrooms) and standard. There's access to the kitchen and free Wi-Fi. A buffet breakfast costs 15zł per person.

RECOMMENDED HOTELS

The following represents a small selection of some of the more interesting places to stay in Kraków and in Tarnów and Zakopane, the two major excursion destinations included in this guide.

Prices indicate a double room including breakfast during the high season, which kicks off around the start of June and finishes towards the end of September. Booking in advance is advisable year-round, and absolutely essential during the high season.

Hotel room rates may be quoted in US dollars, euros and Polish złoty – though the bill will ultimately be rendered in złoty. All establishments listed here accept major credit cards, except where noted.

$$$$	over 600zł
$$$	425–600zł
$$	250–425zł
$	below 250zł

OLD TOWN

Barbican House Apartments $$ *ul. Floriańska 21, tel: 012 346 46 70*, www. barbican-house.com. A range of good-looking modern apartments for up to three persons in the heart of the Old Town, equipped with a good range of amenities, small kitchenettes and Wi-fi. The breakfast is not included and all the apartments are strictly non-smoking. Long-term rents are also available.

Copernicus $$$$ *ul. Kanonicza 16, tel: 012 424 34 00*, https://copernicus. hotel.com.pl. The Copernicus, parts of which date from the 14th century, is located on the city's oldest street and features some breathtaking views of Wawel. Facilities include vast Jacuzzis, a fine restaurant, piano bar, library and a glorious rooftop terrace during the summer. A favourite with visiting VIPs. If you can afford it, this is money well spent indeed – you'll have a truly memorable stay.

Francuski $$$$ *ul. Pijarska 13, tel: 0530 685 192/666 195 831*, www.hotel-francuski.com.pl. This handsome hotel, built in 1912, is on the edge of the Old Town, facing the Planty near the old city wall and the Czartoryski Museum. The hotel is three minutes' walk from the Rynek. Rooms are traditional in style. Wheelchair access.

Grand $$$$ *ul. Sławkowska 5/7, tel: 012 424 08 00*, www.grand.pl. Putting up people in its comfortable beds for over a century, the Grand Hotel, with its wonderfully over-the-top decor, has effortless charm and sophistication. It's the perfect place to celebrate life with all the luxury trimmings, and is well located a short distance from the Rynek. Extras include a magnificently decorated restaurant and café, plus the kind of service that you get only at prices like this.

Hotel Wentzl $$$ *Rynek Główny 9, tel: 012 430 26 64* ; http://wentzl.pl. Ideally situated on the main square in a building that dates back to the 16th century. It boasts spacious, carefully decorated rooms with antique accents (some of them overlooking the square), two excellent restaurants (Wentzl on the first floor and Da Pietro in the cellar, see page) as well as the Słodki Wentzl café on the ground floor. Services include airport pick-up/drop-off, car and bike rental, laundry and ironing. 18 double rooms (discounted rates often available on-line).

Pod Różą $$$$ *ul. Floriańska 14, tel: 012 424 33 00*, https://podroza.hotel.com.pl. An excellent hotel that welcomes you with a sharp click of its automatic wooden doors. The casual-looking reception masks the opulence of the rooms upstairs, which are fitted out with fine antiques as well as the latest gadgets. The hotel also has two restaurants and a vinoteka.

Pollera $$ *ul. Szpitalna 30, tel: 012 422 10 44*, www.pollera.com.pl. A fabulous Art Nouveau masterpiece in an equally good location, the historic Pollera offers surprisingly good value with all the trimmings. It also has a fantastic Wyspiański stained-glass window as its focal point. This is the ideal location for anyone visiting with an eye to the finer things the city has to offer.

Stary $$$$ *ul. Szczepańska 5, tel: 012 384 08 08,* https://stary.hotel.com. pl. Everything is impeccable here, from a renovation job that perfectly melds 14th-century and contemporary style, to staff who are genuinely pleased to help. To top it all, a rooftop bar with a splendid view of the Rynek provides a wonderful place to unwind during the summer.

Wit Stwosz $$ *ul. Mikołajska 28, tel: 012 429 60 26,* http://hotelws.pl. The Wit Stwosz is named after the medieval German master carver whose contributions to the city are many and great. The master clearly didn't have a hand in decorating the rooms here, which are nevertheless tastefully decorated in a style harking back to the glory days of the 19th century. The hotel is very well located in a 16th-century town house just two minutes' walk from the Rynek. As is almost standard throughout the centre of the city, there is a lovely-looking restaurant in a charming brick cellar.

KAZIMIERZ

Eden $$ *ul. Ciemna 15, tel: 012430 65 65,* www.hoteleden.pl. A friendly, small hotel leading a revival of the historic Jewish quarter, Kazimierz. The hotel, before renovation, can be seen in the film Schindler's List. Simple and modern furnishings in a renovated 15th-century building, with a salt-cave sauna, mikvah (Jewish ritual bath) and offering groups who pre-book kosher food.

Tournet $-$$ *ul. Miodowa 7, tel: 012 292 00 88,* www.nocleg.krakow.pl. Cheerful pension accommodation in the heart of Kazimierz, featuring spartan, but comfortable rooms with basic fittings, showers and a kettle. The more expensive rooms are essentially the same, only with a television, which you're probably not going to watch anyway. Good buffet breakfast.

WEST OF THE OLD TOWN

Cybulskiego Guest Rooms $ *ul. Cybulskiego 6, tel: 012 423 05 32,* www. freerooms.pl. A short walk from Rynek Główny, this is a simple, well-run set of rooms and small apartments, all with private bathrooms and kitchenettes, that has a cheerful cellar breakfast room.

Radisson Blu Hotel Krakow $$$ *Ul. Straszewskiego 17, tel: 012 618 88 88*, www.radissonblu.com/hotel-krakow. Swedish-owned and -operated luxury, where the rooms – decorated in pastel shades – are large, and the service is as fussy or as discreet as you want it to be. Bathrooms are a particular treat, with their heated floors, wide range of complimentary cosmetics and super-soft robes. There is, of course, an on-site sauna, good restaurants and a lazy, comfortable lobby bar. Surprisingly affordable.

EAST OF THE OLD TOWN

Best Western Plus Kraków Old Town $$$ *ul. św. Gertrudy 6, tel: 012 422 76 66*, www.bwoldtown.pl. This one-time Commie haunt called the Monopol has been completely modernised and rebranded and is starting to win awards. It now caters mostly to tour groups who favour its combination of pleasant rooms and good facilities, proximity to the Old Town and down-to-earth prices. On a busy tram route and nicely situated between the Old Town and Kazimierz, it can also cater for disabled people.

Topolowa Residence $$ *ul. Topolowa 27, tel: 012 421 01 20*, http://topolowaresidence.pl. This good value residence located in a quiet street near the Old Town, offers five different types of apartments each equipped with a flat-screen television and a kitchenette. The staff are friendly and attentive.

Wielopole $$ *ul. Wielopole 3, tel: 012 422 14 75*, www.wielopole.pl. Another bargain treat midway between the Old Town and Kazimierz. With a nice interior, the Wielopole stands out for the polished attitude of the staff, who can never do enough for you. The rooms are basic, with simple showers, cable television, fridge and free internet in every room. Breakfast is included in the price.

NOWA HUTA

Santorini $$ *ul. Bulwarowa 35b, tel: 012 680 51 95/ 501 160 501*, www.santorinikrakow.pl. If you've got a car or are really interested in Nowa

Huta then the Santorini will be right up your street. Offering very good value, this comfortable hotel in a garden setting features classic mid-range rooms with satellite television, internet access and minibars. The in-house restaurant (see page 112) isn't going to win any awards, but it's by far the best place to eat in the area.

TARNÓW

As with Zakopane, a visit to Tarnów can easily be turned into something longer than a day trip. The three options listed here are the tip of the accommodation iceberg.

Tarnovia \$\$ *ul. Kościuszki 10, tel: 014 630 03 50*, www.hotel.tarnovia.pl. A 1970s-built masterpiece and recommended just for its socialist charm, the Tarnovia has rooms that come in a wide range of options, from simple shoeboxes to spruced-up rooms bordering on business class, to apartments. The recently modernised premium rooms are especially good value. Close to the railway and bus stations.

Tourist Information Centre \$ *Rynek 7, tel: 014 688 90 90*, www.it.tarnow.pl. Tarnów's Tourist Information Centre offers its own guest rooms overlooking the main market square. Rooms are clean and comfortable, cheap and convenient. Having a valuable source of local information downstairs is another good reason to choose this place, as are the unexpected additions, including free wireless internet throughout. This is the best accommodation bargain in town. Credit cards accepted.

U Jana \$ *Rynek 14, tel: 014 626 05 64*, www.hotelujana.pl. An interior that's a peculiar mix of bygone splendour and bling awaits guests of U Jana. The rooms are large, featuring lovely wooden floors, huge double beds and refreshing showers. Guests here enjoy especially value good breakfasts.

ZAKOPANE

Bearing in mind that Zakopane receives 50 times its population in tourists annually, it's vital to book a hotel if you're planning to stay during the high seasons of summer (June–September) or winter (Christmas–March).

Gospoda Pod Niebem $ *ul. Droga Stanisława Zubka 5, tel: 018 206 29 09,* www.podniebem.zakopane.pl. Gospoda Pod Niebem is a charming albeit basic wooden house on top of Gubałówka Hill above Zakopane. Expect little in the way of extras like trouser presses or room service, but do prepare yourself for the invigorating smell of pine, more fresh air than you could ever wish for, and a fantastic view of the Tatras. The rooms come with a bed, television, shower and little else, but for the price and the location you can't really do better.

Grand Hotel Stamary $$$$ *ul. Kościuszki 19, tel: 018 202 45 10,* www.stamary.pl. A strange location next to the bus station for such a fine hotel as this, but from the balconies there is a wonderful view of the Tatras. The Grand has luxurious rooms with all the trimmings, very well-mannered staff, spa facilities and the best espressos in town – you get what you pay for here, which is a lot. The Grand is highly recommended if your budget allows.

Logos $$ *ul. Grunwaldzka 10, tel: 018 263 70 20,* www.logos-zakopane.pl. Located in the centre of Zakopane, this hotel tries to combine unique local tradition with modern amenities. The rooms are simply decorated with elegantly used popular motives. Spa centre, a restaurant serving traditional local cuisine and a third floor view café are additional assets. Good price for the quality offered.

DICTIONARY

ENGLISH–POLISH

adj adjective **adv** adverb **BE** British English **n** noun **prep** preposition **v** verb

A

a little trochę
a lot dużo
a.m. przed południem
accept *v* zaakceptować
accident (road) wypadek
accidentally przypadkowo
across przez
acrylic *adj* akrylowy; *n* akryl
actor aktor
adapter przejściówka
address adres
admission charge opłata za wstęp
adult *n* dorosły
afraid przestraszony
after (time) po; **(place)** za
afternoon popołudnie
aftershave płyn po goleniu
ago temu
agree zgadzać się
air conditioner klimatyzator
air conditioning klimatyzacja
air mattress materac nadmuchiwany
air pump kompresor
airline linia lotnicza
airmail poczta lotnicza
airport lotnisko
air-sickness bag torebka na chorobę lotniczą
aisle seat miejsce przy przejściu

alarm clock budzik
allergic uczulony
allergy uczulenie
allowance ilość
almost prawie
alone sam
already już
also również
alter poprawić
aluminum foil folia aluminiowa
always zawsze
amazing zdumiewający
ambassador ambasador
ambulance karetka
American *adj* amerykański; *n* Amerykanin
amount (money) kwota
and i
anesthetia znieczulenie
animal zwierzę
another inny
antacid środek neutralizujący kwas
antibiotics antybiotyk
antique *n* antyk
antiseptic aseptyczny
antiseptic cream krem aseptyczny
any jakiś
anyone ktoś
apartment mieszkanie
apologize przepraszać

appendix wyrostek robaczkowy
appetite apetyt
appetizer przekąska
appointment (business) spotkanie; **(doctor)** wizyta
approximately około
arcade salon gier
area code numer kierunkowy
arm (body part) ramię
around (time) około; **(place)** po
arrive (car, train) przyjeżdżać; **(plane)** lądować
art gallery galeria sztuki
artist artysta
ashtray popielniczka
ask (question) pytać; **(request)** prosić
aspirin aspiryna
asthma astma
at (time) o; **(place)** na
ATM bankomat
attack atak
attractive atrakcyjny
audioguide przewodnik dźwiękowy
Australia Australia
authenticity autentyczność
automatic trasmission automatycza skrzynia biegów
autumn [BE] jesień
available (free) wolne
avalanche lawina

B

baby dziecko
baby food jedzenie dla dzieci
baby wipe wilgotne chusteczki pielęgnacyjne
babysitter opiekunka
back (head) tył; **(body)** grzbiet
backache ból grzbietu
backpack n plecak; v wędrować z plecakiem
bad zły
bag torba
baggage [BE] bagaż
baggage room przechowalnia bagażu
bakery piekarnia
balcony balkon
ball piłka
ballet balet
band (music) zespół
bandage bandaż
bank bank
bar bar
barber fryzjer męski
basement piwnica
basketball koszykówka
bath n wanna; v kąpiel
bathroom łazienka
battery bateria; **(car)** akumulator
battle site pole bitwy
be być
beach plaża
beautiful piękny
because ponieważ
bed łóżko
bedding pościel
bedroom sypialnia
before (time) przed
begin zaczynać
beginner początkujący
behind za

belong należeć
belt pasek
berth (ship) koja; **(train)** kuszetka
best najlepszy
better lepszy
between pomiędzy
bib śliniaczek
bicycle rower
bicycle route szlak rowerowy
big duży
bikini bikini
bill (restaurant) rachunek
binoculars lornetka
bird ptak
birthday urodziny
bite n ugryzienie
bitter gorzki
bizarre dziwaczny
black czarny
bladder pęcherz moczowy
bland mdły
blanket koc
bleach wybielacz
bleed krwawić
bleeding krwotok
blister pęcherz
block v blokować
blood krew
blood pressure ciśnienie krwi
blouse bluzka
blow-dry suszenie z modelowaniem
blue niebieski
board pokład
boarding card karta pokładowa
boat trip przejażdżka statkiem
boil v gotować
boiler boiler
bone kość
book książka

bookstore księgarnia
boots botki
boring nudny
born v urodzić się
borrow pożyczyć
botanical garden ogród botaniczny
bottle butelka
bottle opener otwieracz do butelek
bowl miska
box (container) pudełko
boy chłopiec
boyfriend chłopak
bra biustonosz
bracelet bransoletka
brake hamulec
break (destroy) zepsuć; **(body part)** złamać
break down (go wrong) zepsuć się
breakfast śniadanie
breast (body) pierś
breathe oddychać
bridge most
briefs (clothing) majtki
bring przenieść
Britain Wielka Brytania
British adj brytyjski; n Brytyjczyk
brochure broszura
broken zepsuty
bronchitis bronchit
brooch broszka
brother brat
browse patrzeć
bruise siniak
bucket wiaderko
bug robak
build budować
building budynek
bulletin board tablica informacyjna

burn *n* oparzenie
bus autobus
bus route trasa autobusowa
bus station dworzec autobusowy
bus stop przystanek autobusowy
business biznes
business class klasa biznes
busy zajęty
but ale
butane gas butan
butcher (store) rzeźnik
button guzik
buy kupić

C

cabaret kabaret
café kawiarnia
call (ambulance) wezwać;
   (telephone) zadzwonić
camera aparat fotograficzny
camera case futerał na aparat
camp *n* obóz; *v* obozować
campfire ognisko
campsite pole namiotowe
can *n* puszka; *v* móc
can opener otwieracz do puszek
Canada Kanada
canal kanał
cancel odwołać
cancer rak
cap (dental) koronka; **(clothing)** czapka
car samochód; **(train)** wagon
car hire [BE] wynajem
   samochodów
car insurance ubezpieczenie
   samochodowe
car park parking
car rental wynajem samochodów
car seat fotelik dziecięcy
carafe karafka
card karta

careful ostrożny
carpet dywan
carry-on (luggage) bagaż
   podręczny
cart wózek
carton karton
cash (money) gotówka;
   v zrealizować
cashier kasjer
casino kasyno
castle zamek
catch (bus) złapać
cathedral katedra
cave jaskinia
CD płyta
CD player odtwarzacz płyt
   kompaktowych
cell phone telefon komórkowy
cemetery cmentarz
ceramics ceramika
certificate certyfikat
chain łańcuszek
change *n* **(small coins)**
   drobne; **(in shop)** reszta; *v*
   (bus, train) przesiąść się;
   (baby) przewinąć; **(money)**
   wymieniać; **(reserva-
   tion)** zmienić, **(clothes)**
   przebrać się
changing room przebieralnia
charcoal węgiel drzewny
charge opłata
cheap tani
check *n* czek
check in *n* odprawa
check out (hotel)
   wyrejestrować się
checkbook książeczka
   czekowa
check-in desk stanowisko
   odprawy
chemical toilet chemiczna

   toaleta
chemist [BE] apteka
cheque [BE] czek
chess szachy
chest (body) klatka persiana
child dziecko
child's cot łóżeczko dziecięce
child's seat krzesełko dla
   dziecka
church kościół
cigar cygaro
cigarette papieros
clamp założyć blokadę na koła
clean *adj* czysty; *v* wyczyścić
cliff klif
cling film [BE] folia do
   żywności
clinic klinika
clock zegar
close (near) niedaleko;
   (store) zamykać
clothing store sklep odzieżowy
cloudy pochmurno
**coach [BE] (long-distance
   bus)** autokar
coat płaszcz
coat check szatnia
coat hanger wieszak
cockroach karaluch
coin moneta
cold *adj* zimny; *adv* zimno; *n*
   (illness) przeziębienie
collapse upaść
collect zebrać
collect call rozmowa na koszt
   rozmówcy
colour kolor
colour film film kolorowy
comb grzebień
come przyjść
come back (return) wrócić
commission prowizja

company (companionship)
towarzystwo; **(business)** firma
compartment (train) przedział
composer kompozytor
computer komputer
concert koncert
concert hall sala koncertowa
concession koncesja
concussion wstrząs mózgu
conditioner odżywka
condom prezerwatywa
conductor dyrygent
confirm potwierdzić
confirmation potwierdzenie
connect (internet) połączyć
się z siecią
connection (train) połączenie
conscious (awake) przytomny
constant ciągły
constipation zaparcie
consulate konsulat
consult skonsultować się
contact skontaktować się
contact lens szkło kontaktowe
contagious zakaźny
contain zawierać
contraceptive środek antykon-
cepcyjny
convenience store sklep
osiedlowy
cook v gotować; n kucharz
cooker [BE] kuchenka
cooking (cuisine) kuchnia
cooking facilities możliwość
gotowania
copper miedź
copy kopia
corkscrew korkociąg
correct prawidłowy
cosmetics kosmetyki
cost v kosztować
cot rozkładane łóżko

cottage domek
cotton (material) bawełna
cough n kaszel; v kaszleć
country kraj
country code numer kierunkowy
country music muzyka country
course (meal) danie; **(path)**
droga
cousin kuzyn
cramp skurcz
credit card karta kredytowa
credit card number numer
karty kredytowej
crib łóżeczko dziecięce
cross v przejść
cross-country skis biegówki
crowd tłok
crowded zatłoczony
crown (dental) koronka;
(royal) korona
cruise n rejs
crystal (quartz) kryształ
cup filiżanka
cupboard szafka kuchenna
currency waluta
currency exchange office
kantor
currency exchange rate kurs
wymiany
curtain zasłona
customs urząd celny
customs declaration
deklaracja celna
cut (hair) strzyżenie; **(wound)**
rana cięta
cut glass cięte szkło
cutlery sztućce
cycling kolarstwo

D

daily adj codzienny; adv
codziennie

damaged zniszczony
damp adj wilgotny
dance n taniec; v tańczyć
dance club dyskoteka
dangerous niebezpieczny
dark ciemny
daughter córka
dawn świt
day dzień
day charge opłata za dzień
day ticket bilet jednodniowy
day trip wycieczka jednodniowa
dead (battery) wyczerpany
deaf głuchy
deck chair leżak
declare zadeklarować
deduct odejmować
deep głęboki
defrost rozmrozić
degree (temperature) stopień
delay opóźnienie
delayed opóźniony
delicatessen delikatesy
delicious smaczny
deliver dostarczyć
delivery dostawa
denim drelich
dental floss nić dentystyczna
dentist dentysta
denture proteza dentystyczna
deodorant dezodorant
depart (train, bus) odjeżdżać;
(plane) startować
department store dom
towarowy
departure lounge poczekalnia
departures (airport) hala
odlotów
deposit (security) kaucja
describe opisać
description opis
destination (travel) cel podróży

detail szczegół
detergent środek czystości
develop (photos) wywołać
diabetes cukrzyca
diabetic n cukrzyk
dialing code numer kierunkowy
diamond brylant
diaper pieluszka
diarrhea biegunka
dice kostka do gry
dictionary słownik
diesel diesel
diet dieta
difficult trudny
dining car wagon restauracyjny
dining room jadalnia
dinner kolacja
direct adj **(train, journey)**
bezpośredni; v **(to a place)**
wskazać kierunek
direction kierunek
director (company) dyrektor
directory (telephone) książka
telefoniczna
dirty brudny
disabled n niepełnosprawny
discount zniżka
discount card karta rabatowa
dish (meal) danie
dishcloth ścierka
dishwasher zmywarka
dishwashing liquid płyn do
zmywania
display cabinet gablota
display case gablota
disposable camera aparat
jednorazowy
disturb przeszkadzać
dive (scuba dive) nurkować;
(jump) skakać
diving equipment sprzęt do
nurkowania

divorced rozwiedziony
dizziness zawroty głowy
do robić
doctor lekarz
doll lalka
dollar dolar
domestic (flight) krajowy
door drzwi
double bed podwójne łóżko
double room pokój dwuo-
sobowy
downtown area centrum
dozen tuzin
dress sukienka
drink (alcoholic) drink; v pić
drink menu lista drinków
drip ciec
drive jechać
driver (car) kierowca
driver's license prawo jazdy
drown tonąć
drugstore drogeria
drunk pijany
dry cleaner's pralnia
chemiczna
dry-clean czyścić **(chemicznie)**
dubbed dubbingowany
dummy [BE] smoczek
during podczas
dustbin [BE] śmietnik
duty cło
duvet kołdra

E

ear ucho
ear drops krople do uszu
earache ból ucha
early adj wczesny; adv wcześnie
earring kolczyk
east wschód
easy łatwy
eat jeść

economy class klasa
turystyczna
elastic adj elastyczny
electric shaver golarka
elektryczna
electrical outlet gniazdko
elektryczne
electronic elektroniczny
elevator winda
e-mail n e-mail; v napisać maila
e-mail address adres e-mail
embassy ambasada
embroidery haft
emerald szmaragd
emergency nagły wypadek
emergency exit wyjście
awaryjne
emergency ward izba przyjęć
empty pusty
enamel emalia
end n koniec; v kończyć (się)
engaged zaręczony
engine silnik
engineer inżynier
England Anglia
English adj angielski; n Anglik
enjoy podobać się
enjoyable przyjemny
enlarge (photos) powiększyć
enough dość
entertainment guide program
rozrywek
entrance fee opłata za wstęp
envelope koperta
epilepsy epilepsja
epileptic n epileptyk
equipment (sports) sprzęt
era epoka
error błąd
escalator schody ruchome
escape route droga
ewakuacyjna

essential niezbędny
e-ticket bilet elektroniczny
eurocheque euroczek
European Union Unia
  Europejska
evening wieczór
evening dress strój wieczorowy
every każdy
examination (medical) badanie
example przykład
except oprócz
excess baggage nadbagaż
exchange wymienić
exchange rate kurs wymiany
excursion wycieczka
exhausted wyczerpany
exit wyjście
expensive drogi
experienced zaawansowany
expiration date data ważności
expiry date [BE] data ważności
exposure (photos)
  naświetlanie
express ekspres
express mail priorytet
extension (phone) wewnętrzny
extra (additional) dodatkowy
extract (tooth) wyrwać
eye oko

F

fabric materiał
face twarz
facial zabieg oczyszczania skóry
faint v zemdleć
fairground wesołe miasteczko
fall n jesień
family rodzina
famous sławny
fan (electric) wentylator
far daleko
farm gospodarstwo

far-sighted dalekowidz
fast szybko
father ojciec
faucet kran
faulty wadliwy
favorite ulubiony
fax faks
fee opłata
feed nakarmić
feel czuć (się)
female kobieta
ferry prom
fever gorączka
few parę
fiancé narzeczony
fiancée narzeczona
field pole
fight (brawl) bójka
fill out (a form) wypełnić
fill up (car) nalać do pełna
filling (dental) plomba
film (camera, movie) film
filter filtr
find znaleźć
fine (well) dobrze; **(penalty)**
  grzywna
finger palec
fire pożar
fire alarm alarm pożarowy
fire brigade [BE] straż pożarna
fire department straż pożarna
fire door drzwi przeciwpożarowe
fire escape schody pożarowe
fire exit wyjście awaryjne
fire extinguisher gaśnica
first class pierwsza klasa
first floor parter
fish store sklep rybny
fit v pasować
fitting room przymierzalnia
fix v naprawić
flame płomień

flashlight latarka
flat (tire) przebity
flavor smak
flea pchła
flea market pchli targ
flight lot
flight number numer lotu
floor (level) piętro
florist kwiaciarnia
flower kwiat
flu grypa
flush (toilet) spuszczać wodę
fly n mucha; v latać
fog mgła
folk art sztuka ludowa
folk music muzyka ludowa
follow (pursue) podążać;
  (road, sign) jechać zgodnie z
food jedzenie
food poisoning zatrucie
  pokarmowe
foot stopa
football [BE] piłka nożna
footpath [BE] dróżka
for (time) przez; **(duration)** na
foreign currency obca waluta
forest las
forget zapominać
fork widelec
form formularz
formal dress strój formalny
fortunately na szczęście
fountain fontanna
foyer (hotel, theater) foyer
fracture złamanie
frame (glasses) oprawka
free (available) wolny; **(without charge)** bezpłatny
freezer zamrażarka
frequently często
fresh świeży
friend przyjaciel

friendly (person) przyjazny; **(place, atmosphere)** przyjemny
frightened przerażony
from (place) z; **(time)** od
front przód
frost mróz
frying pan patelnia
fuel paliwo
full pełny
full board z pełnym wyżywieniem
fun zabawa
funny śmieszny
furniture meble

G

gallon galon
game gra; **(sports)** mecz
garage (mechanic) warsztat samochodowy; **(parking lot)** garaż
garbage śmieci
garbage bag worek na śmieci
garden ogródek
gas (fuel) benzyna
gas station stacja benzynowa
gate (airport) wyjście
gauze gaza
genuine prawdziwy
get (buy) kupić; **(find)** znaleźć
get back (return) wrócić
get off (bus/train) wysiąść
get to dojechać do
gift prezent
gift shop sklep z upominkami
giftwrap zapakować na prezent
girl dziewczyna
girlfriend dziewczyna
give dać
glass (non-alcoholic) szklanka; **(alcoholic)** kieliszek

glasses (optical) okulary
glove rękawiczka
go (on foot) iść; **(by bus, train)** jechać; **(by plane)** lecieć
go away odejść
goggles (swimming) okularki; **(skiing)** gogle
gold złoto
golf golf
golf club kij golfowy
golf course pole golfowe
good dobry
good evening dobry wieczór
good morning dzień dobry
good night dobranoc
goodbye do widzenia
gram gram
grandfather dziadek
grandmother babcia
grandparents dziadkowie
grass trawa
gray szary
great adj świetny; adv świetnie
green zielony
greengrocer [BE] warzywniak
grocery store sklep spożywczy
ground (earth) ziemia
ground floor [BE] parter
groundcloth podłoga namiotu
groundsheet [BE] podłoga namiotu
group grupa
group guide przewodnik grupowy
group leader kierownik grupy
group ticket bilet grupowy
guarantee gwarancja
guest gość
guesthouse pensjonat
guide (tour) przewodnik
guidebook przewodnik
guided tour wycieczka z przewodnikiem
guided walk wycieczka piesza z przewodnikiem
guitar gitara
gym siłownia
gynecologist ginekolog

H

hair włosy
hair gel żel do włosów
haircut strzyżenie włosów
hairdresser fryzjer
hairspray lakier do włosów
half pół
hammer młotek
hand ręka
hand luggage [BE] bagaż podręczny
hand washable prać ręcznie
handbag torebka
handicapped niepełnosprawny
handicrafts wyroby rękodzielnicze
handkerchief chusteczka
hanger wieszak
hangover n kac
happy szczęśliwy
harbor port
hard (texture) twardy; **(difficult)** ciężki
hat kapelusz
have mieć
hay fever katar sienny
head n głowa; v **(go towards)** jechać w kierunku
head waiter kierownik sali
headache ból głowy
health zdrowie
health food store sklep ze zdrową żywnością
health insurance ubezpieczenie zdrowotne

hear słyszeć
hearing aid aparat słuchowy
heart serce; **(cards)** kier
heart attack zawał serca
heat ogrzewanie
heater grzejnik
heating [BE] ogrzewanie
heavy ciężki
height wzrost
helmet kask
help pomoc
hemorrhoids hemoroidy
her jej
here tutaj
hernia przepuklina
herpes opryszczka
hers jej
high wysoki
highchair wysokie krzesełko
highlight v **(hair)** robić pasemka; **(stress)** podkreślić
highway autostrada
hiking (general) turystyka piesza; **(trip)** wędrówka
hill wzgórze
him niego
hire [BE] v wynajać
his jego
historic site miejsce historyczne
hobby (pastime) hobby
holiday [BE] wakacje
holiday resort miejscowość wypoczynkowa
home (be/go) w domu/do domu
honeymoon miesiąc miodowy
horse koń
horse racing wyścigi konne
hospital szpital
hot gorący
hot spring gorące źródło
hotel hotel

hour godzina
house dom
housewife gospodyni domowa
hundred sto
hungry głodny
hurt boleć
husband mąż

I

ice-cream parlor lodziarnia
icy oblodzony
identification dowód tożsamości
ill chory
illegal nielegalny
imitation imitacja
in (place) w; **(period of time)** w ciągu
included wliczony
incredible niewiarygodny
indicate wskazywać
indigestion niestrawność
indoor pool kryty basen
inexpensive niedrogi
infected zakażony
infection infekcja
inflammation zapalenie
informal (dress) nieformalny
information (desk, office) infomacja
injection zastrzyk
injured ranny
innocent niewinny
insect insekt
insect bite ugryzienie owada
insect repellent środek na owady
insect sting użądlenie
inside w środku
insist nalegać
insomnia bezsenność
instead zamiast

instruction instrukcja
instructor instruktor
insulin insulina
insurance ubezpieczenie
insurance card polisa ubezpieczeniowa
insurance certificate [BE] polisa ubezpieczeniowa
insurance claim wniosek o odszkodowanie
interest (hobby) zainteresowanie
interested zainteresowany
interesting interesujący
international (flight) międzynarodowy
International Student Card Międzynarodowa Karta Studenta
internet internet
internet cafe kafejka internetowa
interpreter tłumacz ustny
intersection skrzyżowanie
into do
intolerance nietolerancja
invite zaprosić
iodine jodyna
Ireland Irlandia
iron n żelazko; v prasować
itch swędzieć
item (object) przedmiot
itemized bill szczegółowy rachunek

J

jacket (men's) marynarka; **(women's)** żakiet
jaw szczęka
jazz jazz
jeans dżinsy
jellyfish meduza

jet-ski skuter wodny
jeweler jubiler
jewelry biżuteria
join (a group) dołączyć się
joint (body) staw
joke żart
journalist dziennikarz
journey podróż
jug (water) dzbanek
jumper [BE] pulower
junction [BE] (intersection) skrzyżowanie

K

keep zatrzymać
kerosene nafta
kettle czajnik
key klucz
key card (hotel) karta
kiddie pool brodzik
kidney nerka
kilometer kilometr
kind adj uprzejmy; n rodzaj
kiss n pocałunek; v całować
kitchen kuchnia
kitchen foil [BE] folia aluminiowa
knee kolano
knickers [BE] majtki
knife nóż
know wiedzieć
kosher koszerny

L

label (sticker) nalepka; **(on bottle)** etykieta
lace koronka
ladder drabina
lake jezioro
lamp lampa
land v lądować
language course kurs językowy

large (size) duży
last adj ostatni; **(previous)** zeszły; v trwać
late (not early) późny; **(delayed)** opóźniony
later później
laundromat pralnia samoobsługowa
laundry facilities pralnia
lawyer prawnik
laxative środek przeczyszczający
lead n smycz; v prowadzić
leader (ideological) przywódca; **(manager)** menedżer
leak n przeciek; v **(roof, pipe)** przeciekać
learn (language) uczyć się
leather skóra
leave (depart) odjeżdżać; **(deposit)** zostawić; **(on foot)** odejść; **(depart of plane)** odlatywać
left adj lewy
left-luggage office [BE] przechowalnia bagażu
leg noga
legal legalny
lend pożyczyć
lens (optical) soczewka; **(camera)** obiektyw
lense cap nakładka na obiektyw
less mniej
lesson lekcja
let v **(permit)** pozwolić
let go puścić
letter list
library biblioteka
license plate number numer rejestracyjny
life preserver koło ratunkowe

lifeboat łódź ratunkowa
lifeguard ratownik
lifejacket kamizelka ratunkowa
lift [BE] winda
lift pass (skiing) skipass
light adj **(weight)** lekki; **(colour)** jasny; n światło
light bulb żarówka
lighter adj jaśniejszy; n zapalniczka
like v lubić
limousine limuzyna
line (metro) linia metra
linen len
lip warga
lipgloss błyszczyk
lipstick szminka
liquor store sklep monopolowy
liter litr
little (small) mały
live mieszkać
liver wątroba
living room salon
lobby (theater) foyer; **(hotel)** hol
local lokalny
lock n **(door)** zamek; **(bike)** blokada; v zamknąć
log off wylogować się
log on zalogować się
login login
long długi
long-distance bus autokar
long-sighted [BE] dalekowidz
loose luźny
lorry [BE] ciężarówka
lose (item) zgubić; **(person)** stracić
lost-and-found biuro rzeczy znalezionych
lost-property office [BE] biuro rzeczy znalezionych

love *n* miłość; *v* kochać
lovely śliczny
low niski
lower (berth) dolny
low-fat o niskiej zawartości tłuszczu
luck szczęście
luggage bagaż
luggage cart wózek na bagaż
luggage locker schowek na bagaż
luggage trolley [BE] wózek na bagaż
lump guz
lunch obiad
lung płuco

M

machine washable prać w pralce
madam pani
magazine czasopismo
magnificent wspaniały
maid pokojówka
mail *n* poczta; *v* wysłać
mailbox skrzynka pocztowa
main główny
make zrobić
male mężczyzna
mallet młotek drewniany
manager menadżer
manicure manicure
many dużo
map mapa
market (job market) rynek; **(place to buy)** targ
married żonaty
mascara tusz do rzęs
mask (diving) maska
mass msza
massage masaż
match (game) mecz; **(light)**

zapałka
mattress materac
maybe może
me ja
meal posiłek
measles odra
measure zmierzyć
measurement miara
measuring cup miarka kuchenna
measuring spoon łyżka do odmierzania
mechanic mechanik
medication lek
medicine lekarstwo
medium średni
meet (get to know) poznać; **(appointment)** spotkać
meeting place miejsce zbiórki
meeting point [BE] miejsce zbiórki
member (association) członek
memorial (war) pomnik
mention wspominać
menu menu
message wiadomość
metal metal
metro map mapa metra
metro station stacja metra
microwave (oven) kuchenka mikrofalowa
midday [BE] południe
midnight północ
migraine migrena
million milion
mine mój
mini-bar mini-bar
minute (time) minuta
mirror lustro
miss (lack) brakować; **(lost)** zaginąć
mistake błąd

misunderstanding nieporozumienie
mobile home przyczepa mieszkalna
mobile phone [BE] telefon komórkowy
moisturizer (cream) krem nawilżający
monastery klasztor
money pieniądze
money order przekaz pieniężny
month miesiąc
monument pomnik
mop mop
moped motorower
more więcej
morning rano
mosque meczet
mosquito bite ukąszenie komara
mother matka
motion sickness choroba lokomocyjna
motorbike motor
motorboat motorówka
motorcycle motor
motorway [BE] autostrada
mountain góra
mountain bike rower górski
mountain pass przełęcz górska
mountain range łańcuch górski
moustache wąsy
mouth usta
move ruszać
movie film
movie theater kino
much dużo
mug *n* kubek; *v* napadać
mugging napad
mumps świnka

muscle mięsień
museum muzeum
music muzyka
music store sklep muzyczny
musician muzyk
must *v* musieć
my mój

N

name imię
napkin serwetka
nappy [BE] pieluszka
narrow wąski
national narodowy
national park park narodowy
nationality obywatelstwo
native tutejszy
nature reserve rezerwat przyrody
nature trail szlak przyrodniczy
nausea mdłości
near niedaleko
nearby niedaleko
near-sighted krótkowidz
necessary konieczny
neck (body) szyja
necklace naszyjnik
need *v* potrzebować
nerve nerw
nervous system układ nerwowy
never nigdy
new nowy
newsagent [BE] kiosk z gazetami
newspaper gazeta
newsstand kiosk z gazetami
next następny
nice miły
night noc
night club klub nocny
no nie
noisy hałaśliwy

none żaden
nonsense bzdura
non-smoking *adj* dla niepalących
noon południe
normal normalny
north północ
nose nos
nothing nic
notify zawiadomić
now teraz
number numer
nurse pielęgniarka
nylon nylon

O

occasionally czasami
occupied zajęty
office (place) biuro
off-licence [BE] sklep monopolowy
often często
okay okay
old stary
old town stare miasto
on (day, date) w
once raz
one jeden
one-way w jedną stonę
one-way ticket bilet w jedną stronę
open *adj* otwarty; *v* otwierać
opening hours godziny otwarcia
opera opera
opera house opera
operation operacja
opposite naprzeciwko
optician optyk
or albo
orange (colour) pomarańczowy

order *n* zamówienie; *v* zamówić
our(s) nasz
outdoor pool basen otwarty
outrageous (price) horrendalny
outside na zewnątrz
oval owalny
oven piekarnik
overcharge *v* policzyć za dużo
overheat przegrzać się
overnight na noc
owe być dłużnym
own *adj* własny
owner właściciel

P

p.m. po południu
pacifier smoczek
pack pakować
package przesyłka
paddling pool [BE] brodzik
padlock kłódka
pail (toy) wiaderko
pain ból
painkiller środek przeciwbólowy
paint *v* malować
painter malarz
painting obraz
pair para
palace pałac
panorama panorama
pants spodnie
pantyhose rajstopy
paper napkin serwetka papierowa
paper towel ręcznik papierowy
paracetamol [BE] paracetamol
paralysis paraliż
parcel [BE] paczka
parent rodzic
park *n* park; *v* parkować
parking garage parking podziemny

parking lot parking
parking meter parkometr
parliament building budynek parlamentu
partner partner
party (social) przyjęcie
passenger pasażer
passport paszport
passport number numer paszportu
password hasło
pastry shop sklep cukierniczy
patch załatać
patient *n* pacjent
pavement [BE] chodnik
pay płacić
pay phone automat telefoniczny
payment zapłata
peak szczyt
pearl perła
pedestrian pieszy
pedestrian crossing przejście dla pieszych
pedestrian zone strefa zamknięta do ruchu kołowego
peg [BE] spinacz do bielizny
pen długopis
per za
perhaps być może
period (time) okres; **(menstrual)** miesiączka
person osoba
petrol [BE] benzyna
petrol station [BE] stacja benzynowa
pewter cyna
pharmacy apteka
phone *n* telefon; *v* dzwonić
phone card karta telefoniczna
photo zdjęcie
photocopier kopiarka
photograph zdjęcie

photographer fotograf
phrase zwrot
phrase book rozmówki
pick up odebrać
picnic piknik
picnic area miejsce piknikowe
piece (item) sztuka; **(amount)** kawałek
pill (contraceptive) pigułka antykoncepcyjna; **(tablet)** tabletka
pillow poduszka
pillow case poszewka na poduszkę
pink różowy
pipe (smoking) fajka
pitch (camping) pole namiotowe
pizzeria pizzeria
place miejsce
plan *n* plan; *v* planować
plane samolot
plant (greenery) roślina
plaster [BE] plaster
plastic *adj* plastikowy
plastic bag torebka plastikowa
plastic wrap folia spożywcza
plate talerz
platform peron; **[BE]** tor
platinum platyna
play *n* (theater) sztuka; *v* grać
playground plac zabaw
playing field boisko
pleasant przyjemny
please proszę
plug zatyczka
plunger przepychacz
pneumonia zapalenie płuc
point wskazać
poison trucizna
Poland Polska
police policja
police report raport policyjny

police station komisariat policji
Polish *adj* polski; *n* Polak
pollen count stężenie pyłków w powietrzu
polyester poliester
pond staw
pop (music) pop
popular popularny; **(well-known)** znany
port (harbor) port
porter bagażowy
portion porcja
possible możliwy
post [BE] *n* (mail) poczta; *v* wysłać
post office poczta
postage opłata
postcard pocztówka
poster plakat
pot (for cooking) garnek; **(for tea)** dzbanek
pottery ceramika
pound (sterling) funt
powdery (snow) puszysty
power (electricity) prąd
precipice przepaść
pregnant w ciąży
prescribe przepisać
prescription recepta
present (gift) prezent
press naciskać
pretty ładny
price cena
print *n* sztych; *v* drukować
prison więzienie
produce store sklep spożywczy
profession zawód
program program
pronounce wymawiać
pub pub
public *n* publiczność;

adj publiczny
pump (gas station) pompa
puncture przebicie
pure czysty
purple fioletowy
purse torebka
push-chair [BE] wózek spacerowy
put włożyć

Q

quality jakość
quarter ćwierć; **(time)** kwadrans
queue [BE] *n* kolejka; *v* stać w kolejce
quick szybki
quickly szybko
quiet cichy

R

race course [BE] tor wyścigowy
racetrack tor wyścigowy
racket (tennis, squash) rakieta
railway station [BE] stacja kolejowa
rain *n* deszcz
raincoat płaszcz przeciwdeszczowy
rape *n* gwałt; *v* zgwałcić
rapids progi rzeczne
rare (unusual) rzadki
rash wysypka
razor maszynka do golenia
razor blade żyletka
read *v* czytać
ready gotowy
real (genuine) prawdziwy
rear tylny
receipt paragon
receive odebrać

reception (desk) recepcja
receptionist recepcjonista
recommend polecić
red czerwony
reduction (price) obniżka
refrigerator lodówka
refund zwrot pieniędzy
region (area) region
registered mail list polecony
registration form formularz rejestracji
reliable niezawodny
religion religia
remember pamiętać
rent wynająć
rental car wynajęty samochód
repair *n* naprawa; *v* naprawić
repeat powtórzyć
replacement wymiana
replacement part część zamienna
report (crime) zgłosić
require wymagać
reservation rezerwacja
reservations desk okienko rezerwacji
reserve *v* rezerwować
rest *v* odpoczywać
restaurant restauracja
restroom toaleta
return wrócić; **(surrender)** zwrócić
return ticket [BE] bilet powrotny
reverse-charge call [BE] rozmowa na koszt rozmówcy
rheumatism reumatyzm
rib żebro
right (correct) poprawny; **(good)** dobry
right of way pierwszeństwo przejazdu

ring pierścionek
river rzeka
road droga
road map mapa drogowa
road sign znak drogowy
rob obrabować
robbery rabunek
rock (music) rock; **(land formation)** skała
romantic romantyczny
roof dach
roof-rack bagażnik dachowy
room (hotel) pokój
room service room service
rope lina
round okrągły
round-trip ticket bilet powrotny
route trasa
rubbish [BE] śmieci
rude niegrzeczny
ruins ruiny

S

safe *adj* bezpieczny; *n* sejf
safety bezpieczeństwo
safety pin agrafka
sand piasek
sandal sandał
sanitary napkin podpaska
sanitary pad [BE] podpaska
satellite TV telewizja satelitarna
satin satyna
saucepan rondel
sauna sauna
say *v* powiedzieć
scarf szalik
scissors nożyczki
Scotland Szkocja
screwdriver śrubokręt
sea morze

seasickness choroba moska
season ticket bilet okresowy
seat (train) miejsce
seat reservation (train) miejscówka
second class druga klasa
secondhand store sklep z używaną odzieżą
secretary sekretarka
sedative środek uspokajający
see (spot) zobaczyć; **(inspect)** sprawdzić; **(observe, witness)** widzieć
self-employed samozatrudniony
self-service (gas station) samoobsługa
sell sprzedawać
send wysłać
senior citizen emeryt
separated w separacji
separately osobno
serious poważny
service (in restaurant) obsługa; **(religious)** nabożeństwo
sex seks; **(gender)** płeć
shade odcień
shady cienisty
shallow płytki
shampoo szampon
share v dzielić
sharp ostry
shaving cream krem do golenia
she ona
sheet (bed) prześcieradło
shirt (men's) koszula; **(women's)** bluzka
shock (electric) porażenie
shoe but
shoe repair naprawa obuwia
shoe store sklep z obuwiem

shop assistant sprzedawca
shopping area centrum handlowe
shopping basket koszyk
shopping cart wózek
shopping centre [BE] centrum handlowe
shopping mall centrum handlowe
shopping trolley [BE] wózek
short adj **(length)** krótki; **(person)** niski
shorts (clothing) szorty
short-sighted [BE] krótkowidz
shoulder bark
shovel (toy) łopatka
show n **(presentation)** pokaz; **(theater)** sztuka; v pokazać
shower prysznic
shrine kapliczka
shut v zamykać; adj zamknięty
shutter okiennica
side (head) bok
side order dodatek
side street boczna uliczka
sidewalk chodnik
sights atrakcje turystyczne
sightseeing tour wycieczka po mieście
sign znak
silk jedwab
silver srebro
singer pieśniarz
single sam
single room pokój jednoosobowy
single ticket bilet w jedną stronę
sink zlew
sir pan
sister siostra
sit siadać

size rozmiar
skate łyżwa
skewer rożen
ski narta
ski boot but narciarski
ski pole kijek
skin skóra
skirt spódnica
sleep spać
sleeper car [BE] wagon sypialny
sleeping bag śpiwór
sleeping car wagon sypialny
sleeping pill tabletka nasenna
sleeve rękaw
slice plasterek
slip v poślizgnąć się
slipper pantofel
slow wolny
slowly wolno
small mały
smell pachnieć
smoke palić
smoking (area) dla palących
snack przekąska
snack bar bar
sneaker tenisówka
snorkel fajka do nurkowania
snow śnieg
soap mydło
soccer piłka nożna
sock skarpetka
socket gniazdko
sole (shoes) podeszwa
some jakiś
something coś
sometimes czasami
somewhere gdzieś
son syn
soon niedługo
sore throat ból gardła
sorry przepraszam

soul (music) soul
sour kwaśne
south południe
souvenir pamiątka
souvenir store sklep z pamiątkami
spa spa
space miejsce
spare zapasowy
speak mówić
special specjalny
specialist specjalista
specimen próbka
spell v przeliterować
spend (time) spędzać; **(money)** wydawać
spicy ostry
sponge gąbka
spoon łyżka
sport sport
sporting goods store sklep sportowy
spot (place, site) miejsce
sprained skręcony
spring wiosna
square kwadrat
stadium stadion
staff personel
stain plama
stainless steel stal nierdzewna
stairs schody
stamp (postal) znaczek
standby ticket tani bilet okazyjny
start v **(begin)** zaczynać się; **(car)** zapalić
starter [BE] przekąska
statement (police) zeznanie
stationery store sklep papierniczy
statue pomnik
stay n pobyt; v zostać; **(in a hotel)** zatrzymać się
sterilizing solution płyn do sterylizacji
still adv wciąż
stockings [BE] pończochy
stolen ukradziony
stomach brzuch
stomachache ból brzucha
stop n **(bus, tram)** przystanek; v zatrzymywać się
store sklep
store guide tablica informacyjna
storm burza
stove kuchenka
strange dziwny
straw (drinking) słomka
stream strumień
strong (powerful) silny
student student
study v studiować
style styl
subtitled z napisami
suggest zasugerować
suit (men's) garnitur; **(women's)** kostium
suitable stosowny
suitcase walizka
summer lato
sunbathe opalać się
sunburn oparzenie słoneczne
sunglasses okulary słoneczne
sunny słoneczny
sunshade parasol
sunstroke udar słoneczny
suntan lotion krem do opalania
superb znakomity
supermarket supermarket
supervision nadzór
supplement opłata dodatkowa
suppository czopek
sure pewien
surfboard deska do serfowania

surname nazwisko
sweater sweter
sweatshirt bluza
sweet (taste) słodki
swelling opuchlizna
swim pływać
swimming pool basen
swimming trunks kąpielówki
swimsuit kostium kąpielowy
swollen spuchnięty
symptom (illness) objaw
synagogue synagoga

T

table stolik
take brać; **(carry)** zanieść; **(medicine)** brać; **(time)** trwać
take away [BE] na wynos
talk rozmawiać
tall wysoki
tampon tampon
tan opalenizna
tap [BE] kran
tapestry kilim
taxi taksówka
taxi rank [BE] postój taksówek
taxi stand postój taksówek
teacher nauczyciel
team drużyna
teaspoon łyżeczka do herbaty
teddy bear miś
telephone n telefon; v dzwonić
telephone bill rachunek telefoniczny
telephone booth budka telefoniczna
telephone call rozmowa telefoniczna
telephone number numer telefonu
tell powiedzieć

temperature temperatura
temple świątynia
temporarily tymczasowo
tennis tenis
tennis court kort tenisowy
tent namiot
tent peg kołek
tent pole maszt namiotowy
terminal terminal
terrace taras
terrible okropny
terrific wspaniały
tetanus tężec
text *n* **(phone)** sms;
   (document) tekst
thank *v* dziękować
thank you dziękuję
that to
theater teatr
theft kradzież
their(s) ich
theme park tematyczny park
   rozrywki
then (time) wtedy
there tam
thermometer termometr
these ci
they oni
thick gruby
thief złodziej
thigh udo
thin chudy
think myśleć
thirsty spragniony
this (one) ten
those tamci
thousand tysiąc
throat gardło
through przez
thumb kciuk
ticket bilet
ticket office kasa biletowa

tie krawat
tight *adv* ciasny
tights (clothing) rajstopy
time czas; **(exact time)**
   godzina
timetable [BE] rozkład jazdy
tin opener [BE] otwieracz do
   puszek
tire (car) opona
tired zmęczony
tissue chusteczka
to do
tobacco tytoń
tobacconist sklep tytoniowy
today dzisiaj
toe palec u nogi
toilet [BE] toaleta
toilet paper papier toaletowy
tomorrow jutro
tongue język
tonight dziś wieczorem
too (extreme) za
tooth ząb
toothache ból zęba
toothbrush szczoteczka do
   zębów
toothpaste pasta do zębów
top (head) góra
torn naderwany
tour wycieczka
tour guide przewodnik wycieczki
tour operator organizator
   wycieczki
tourist turysta
tourist office biuro informacji
   turystycznej
tow truck pomoc drogowa
towel ręcznik
tower wieża
town miasto
town center centrum
town hall ratusz

toy zabawka
track tor
traditional tradycyjny
traffic ruch
traffic jam korek
traffic light światła
traffic violation wykroczenie
   drogowe
trailer przyczepa
train pociąg
train station dworzec kolejowy
trained wykwalifikowany
tram tramwaj
transit (travel) przejazd
translate tłumaczyć
translation tłumaczenie
translator tłumacz
trash (garbage) śmieci
trash can śmietnik
travel *n* podróż; *v* podróżować
travel agency biuro podróży
travellers check czek
   podróżny
travellers cheque [BE] czek
   podróżny
tray taca
tree drzewo
trim *v* podstrzyc
trip wycieczka
trolley wózek
trousers spodnie
truck ciężarówka
true prawdziwy
try próbować
try on (clothes) przymierzyć
T-shirt t-shirt
tumor nowotwór
tunnel tunel
turn skręcić
turn down zmniejszyć
turn off wyłączyć
turn on włączyć

turn up (volume, heat) zwiększyć
TV telewizor
tweezers pinceta
twice dwa razy
twin bed łóżko podwójne
twist *v* (hurt) skręcić
type (sort) rodzaj
typical typowy
tyre [BE] opona

U

U.K. Wielka Brytania
U.S. Stany Zjednoczone
ugly brzydki
ulcer wrzód
umbrella parasol
uncle wuj
uncomfortable niewygodny
unconscious nieprzytomny
under pod

understand rozumieć
underwear bielizna
undress rozbierać (się)
uneven (ground) nierówny
unfortunately niestety
uniform mundur
unit (phone card) impuls
university uniwersytet
unleaded (gas) bezołowiowa
unlimited mileage bez limitu kilometrów
unlock otworzyć
unpleasant niemiły
unscrew odkręcić
urgent pilny

V

vacation wakacje
vacuum cleaner odkurzacz
vegetarian *adj* wegetariański;
n wegetarianin
visa wiza

W

wait czekać
wallet portfel
water woda
week tydzień
where gdzie
white biały
window okno
window seat siedzenie przy oknie
wine list lista win
wireless bezprzewodowy
work *v* (function) działać;
(job) pracować

X

X-ray rentgen

POLISH–ENGLISH

A

aktualny up-to-date
alarm przeciwpożarowy fire alarm
aleja boulevard
ambasada embassy
angielski English
Anglia England
antyki antiques store
aparat fotograficzny camera
apteka pharmacy
artykuły bezcłowe duty-free goods
aseptyczny antiseptic
astma asthma

atrakcja turystyczna tourist attraction
autokar long-distance bus [coach *BE*]
autostrada highway [motorway *BE*]

B

bagaż baggage
bagaż podręczny carry-on [hand luggage *BE*]
bagno marsh
balkon balcony (theater)
balsam po opalaniu after-sun lotion

bankomat ATM
basen dla dzieci children's pool
basen kryty indoor swimming pool
basen odkryty outdoor swimming pool
benzyna gas [petrol *BE*]
bez cukru sugar-free
bez tłuszczu fat-free
bezglutenowy gluten-free
bezołowiowy unleaded (gasoline)
bezprzewodowy wireless (internet)
bezzwrotny non-returnable

biblioteka library
biegać v run
biegówki cross-coutry skis
bielizna underwear
bilet ticket
bilet elektroniczny e-ticket
bilet grupowy group ticket
bilet okresowy season ticket
bilet parkingowy parking ticket
biuro office
biuro obsługi klienta
customer service
biuro podróży travel agency
biuro rzeczy znalezionych
lost-and-found [lost-property
office BE]
biuro turystyczne tourist office
biznes business
biżuteria jewelry
błąd mistake
blokada lock (on a bike)
błyszczyk lipgloss
ból pain
budka autobusowa bus shelter
bungalow bungalow
but shoe
butelka bottle

C

cena price
centrum biznesu business
district
centrum handlowe shopping
mall [centre BE]
centrum miasta downtown
area [town centre BE]
**centrum odnowy biologic-
znej** spa
centrum ogrodnicze garden
center
chemiczna toaleta chemical
toilet

chodnik sidewalk [pavement BE]
ciepły warm (water)
ciężarówka truck
ciężki heavy (luggage)
cło duty (customs)
cmentarz cemetery
cukiernia pastry shop
czasopismo magazine
czek check [cheque BE]
czek podróżny travellers
check [cheque BE]
czekać wait

D

dabingowany dubbed
dania dnia menu of the day
darowizna donation
data urodzenia date of birth
data ważności expiration
[expiry BE] date
dawkowanie dosage
deklaracja celna customs
declaration
delikatesy delicatessen
deska do windsurfingu
windsurfing board
deska surfingowa surfboard
dieta diet
długopis pen
do until
do wynajęcia for rent [hire BE]
do żucia chewable (tablets)
dokładna reszta exact change
dom mieszkalny apartment
building
dom towarowy department
store
domowej roboty homemade
dostawa delivery
dostęp access
dowód tożsamości identification

dozorca caretaker
drewno wood
droga road
drzewo tree
drzwi automatyczne
automatic doors
drzwi przeciwpożarowe
fire door
dworzec autobusowy bus
station
dworzec kolejowy train station
dzbanek pot (for tea)
działać v work
działanie uboczne side effect
dziecko child
dzień day
dzień powszedni weekday
dzisiaj today

E

e-mail e-mail
emeryt senior citizen
epilepsja epilepsy
epileptyk epileptic

F

fabryka factory
fajerwerk firework
faks fax
festyn fair
filharmonia concert hall
filiżanka cup
folia aluminiowa aluminum
[kitchen BE] foil
formularz form
fotelik dziecięcy car seat
fryzjer hairdresser
funt pound (sterling)

G

gabinet dentystyczny dental
office [surgery BE]

gabinet lekarski doctor's office [surgery *BE*]
galeria gallery
garnek pot (for cooking)
gaśnica fire extinguisher
gdzie where
giełda stock exchange
głęboko deep
godzina hour
godziny urzedowania business hours
godziny wizyt visiting hours
góra mountain
gorączka temperature
gość guest
gospodarstwo farm
gotować *v* boil
gotówka cash

H

hala targowa indoor market
hamulec bezpieczeństwa emergency brake
hasło password

I

ile how many, how much
imię name
informacja information desk
informacja dla klientów customer information
informacja o lotach flight information
informacja o sklepie store directory [guide *BE*]
instruktor instructor
internet internet
izba przyjęć emergency ward

J

jadalnia dining room
jakość quality

jaskinia cave
jasny light (colour)
jeden one
jedwab silk
jedzenie na wynos to go [take-away *BE*] (food)
jesień fall [autumn *BE*]
jeść eat
jezioro lake
jeździectwo horseback riding
język tongue (part of body); language
język obcy foreign language
jubiler jeweler
jutro tomorrow

K

kafejka internetowa internet cafe
kamizelka ratunkowa life jacket
kantor currency exchange office
kapliczka shrine
kapsułka capsule (medication)
karetka ambulance
karta do telefonu phone card
karta kredytowa credit card
karta pokładowa boarding pass (airport)
karta rabatowa discount card
karta win wine list
kasa biletowa ticket office
kasa ekspresowa express checkout
kasjer cashier
kask crash helmet
katedra cathedral
kaucja deposit
kawałek piece
klieliszek glass (alcoholic)
kierownik manager

kierunek direction (map)
kilometr kilometer
kiosk z gazetami newsstand
klasa biznes business class
klasa turystyczna economy class
klif cliff
klimatyzacja air conditioning
klimatyzator air conditioner
klinika clinic
kolejka linowa cable car
koło ratunkowe life preserver [belt *BE*]
komiks comic book
komisariat police station
kompresor air pump (gas station)
komputer computer
koncert concert
konkurs contest
kontaktować *v* contact
kontrola celna customs control
kontroler biletów ticket inspector
korek traffic jam
kościół church
kosmetyki cosmetics
koszerny kosher
kosztować *v* cost
koszyk shopping basket
kradzież theft
krajowy domestic (flight)
kran faucet [tap *BE*]
krem nawilżający moisturizer
krem z blokadą UV sunscreen
kropla drop (medication)
krwotok bleeding
książka telefoniczna directory
księgarnia bookstore
kucharz cook, chef
kuchenka mikrofalowa microwave

kuchnia kitchen
kurs wymiany exchange rate
kuszetka berth (train)
kwiaciarnia florist
kwiat flower
kwota amount (money)

L

lądować arrive (plane)
las forest
latarnia morska lighthouse
lato summer
lecieć v fly
lekarz doctor
lekki light (weight)
leżak deck chair
linia (lotnicza) airline
list polecony registered letter
list priorytetowy express
   mail
lista drinków drink menu
lokalny local
lot flight
loteria lottery
lotnisko airport
lotnisko krajowe domestic
   airport
lotnisko międzynarodowe
   international airport
lubić v like

Ł

łazienka bathroom
łopatka spatula
łódź ratunkowa life boat
łóżeczko dziecięce crib
   [child's cot BE]
łóżko bed
łyżka do odmierzania
   measuring spoon
łyżwiarstwo ice skating
łyżwy ice skates

M

mały small (size)
mapa drogowa road map
matka mother
mdłości nausea
mdły bland
meble furniture
mgła fog
miarka kuchenna measuring
   cup
miejsce seat (bus, train, plane)
miejsce na piknik picnic area
miejsce przy oknie window
   seat
miejsce przy przejściu
   aisle seat
miejsce urodzenia place
   of birth
miejsce zbiórki meeting place
   [point BE]
miejscówka reservation (train)
międzynarodowy international
mikrofalówka mircowave
miska bowl
mleczarnia dairy
młodzież youth
młyn windmill
mniej less
moczary swamp
mokry wet
mop mop
morze sea
motor motorcycle
motorower moped
mówić speak
msza mass
muzeum museum
mydło soap

N

na dole downstairs
na górze upstairs

na zewnątrz outside
nadbagaż excess baggage
namiot tent
napad mugging
napisać write
napiwek tip
naprawa n repair (car)
naprawić v fix (a car)
narty wodne water skis
następny next
nawierzchnia road surface
nawilżacz moisturizer
nazwisko last name
nazwisko panieńskie maiden
   name
niedaleko close
niepalący non-smoking
nierówny uneven (surface)
noc night
nocleg accommodation
nocny dyżur night duty
nocny portier night porter
normalny normal
nowy new
numer kierunkowy country
   code
numer lotu flight number
numer miejsca seat number
numer pierwszej pomocy
   emergency number

O

objazd detour [diversion BE]
obóz n camp
obozować v camp
od from (time)
odbiór bagażu baggage claim
oddział department
odebrać receive
odkurzacz vacuum cleaner
odlatywać leave
odprawa check-in (airport)

odprawa bagażu baggage check

odwołany cancelled

odzież damska ladieswear

odzież męska menswear

ognisko campfire

ograniczenie prędkości speed limit

ogród garden

okazja bargain

okno window

okres period (of time); menstruation

okulary glasses (optical)

okulary przeciwsłoneczne sunglasses

opera opera

opis description

opłata bankowa bank charge

opłata obowiązkowa minimum charge

opłata za dzień day charge

opłata za usługę service charge

opłata za wstęp admission charge

opóźniony delayed

optyk optician

ostry spicy

ostrzeżenie warning

otwarty open (shop)

P

paczka package [parcel BE]

paczka ekspresowa express mail

pakować pack

palacz smoker

paliwo fuel

pan sir

pani madam

panie ladies (toilet)

panna miss

panowie gentlemen (toilet)

papierowy ręcznik paper towel

paragon receipt

parasol umbrella [sunshade BE]

park narodowy national park

park publiczny public park

parking parking lot [car park BE]

parking podziemny underground garage

parking wielopoziomowy parking garage

parkometr parking meter

parkować v park

parter first floor [ground floor BE]; orchestra [stalls BE] (theater)

pas lane

pasażer passenger

pasmo górskie mountain range

pawilon pavilion

pchać push

pchli targ flea market

peron platform

piasek sand

pić v drink

piekarnia bakery

pielęgniarka nurse

pieniądze money

pierwsza klasa first class

pierwsza pomoc emergency services; first aid

pierwsze piętro second floor [first floor BE]

pieszy pedestrian

piętro floor (level in building)

pigułka pill

pikantny spicy

pilny urgent

pismo periodical

piwnica basement

plac square

plasterek slice

plaża dla nudystów nudist beach

plecak backpack

plomba filling (dental)

płacić v pay

płeć sex (gender)

płyta kompaktowa CD

płytki adj shallow

pływać v swim

po południu p.m.

pociąg Intercity Intercity train

pociąg lokalny local train

początkujący beginner

poczekalnia waiting room

poczta post office

podarunek gift

podjazd ramp

podłoga floor

podobać się like

podpaska sanitary napkin [pad BE]

podróż powrotna round-trip [return trip BE] (ticket)

poduszka pillow

pokład deck (ship)

pokoje do wynajęcia rooms for rent [to let BE]

pokój room (hotel)

pole field

pole bitwy battle site

pole namiotowe camping

polecać recommend

policja police

policja drogowa traffic police

polisa ubezpieczeniowa insurance card [certificate BE]

Polska Poland

południe noon (time); south (direction)
pomiędzy between
pomnik monument
pomoc drogowa breakdown services
poranek morning
port port
portfel wallet
postój taksówek taxi stand [rank *BE*]
pościel sheets
potrzebny required
potwierdzenie confirmation
potwierdzić confirm
powiedzieć *v* say
powtórzyć repeat
poznać meet
pożar fire
północ midnight (time); north (direction)
półwysep peninsula
pracować *v* work
prać oddzielnie wash separately
prać ręcznie hand wash only
pralnia laundry
pralnia chemiczna dry-cleaner
prasować *v* iron
prawnik lawyer
prawo jazdy driver's license
priorytet express mail
progi rzeczne rapids
prognoza pogody weather forecast
prom ferry
proszę please
prowizja commission
prysznic shower
prywatny private
przebieralnia fitting room

przecena sale
przechowalnia bagażu baggage office
przeciek leak
przed before
przed południem a.m.
przedstawić introduce (someone)
przedział compartment
przejście path; aisle (plane)
przejście dla pieszych pedestrian crossing
przejście podziemne underpass
przejściówka adapter
przekaz pieniężny money order
przekąska appetizer [starter *BE*]
przepaść precipice
przepychacz plunger
przesiadać się change [transfer *BE*] (bus)
przesyłka package
przeszkadzać disturb
przetłumaczyć translate
przewodnik guide (person); guidebook
przyczepa trailer
przyloty arrivals (airport)
przymierzalnia fitting room
przystanek autobusowy bus stop
przystanek na żądanie on-demand stop
ptak bird
punkt widzenia view point
pusty vacant

R

rabat discount
ratownik lifeguard

ratusz town hall
recepta prescription
recycling recycling
ręcznie robione handmade
ręcznik towel
rejs cruise
reklama advertisment
rentgen X-ray
restauracja restaurant
reszta *n* change (money)
rezerwacja reservation
rezerwuar reservoir
robak bug
rogatka toll booth
rondel saucepan
rondo roundabout
room service room service
rower bicycle
rozkład jazdy schedule [timetable *BE*]
rozkładane łóżko cot
rozmowa na koszt rozmówcy collect call [reverse-charge call *BE*]
rozumieć understand
rura pipe (water)
rząd row (of seats, people)
rzeka river
rzeźnik butcher

S

sąd courthouse
sala hall (large public room)
sala konferencyjna conference hall
sala zebrań convention hall
salon gier arcade
sam alone
samolot plane
sauna sauna
schowek na bagaż luggage locker

schronisko młodzieżowe youth hostel
ściana wall
ścieżka path
sekretarka secretary
serwetka napkin
sieć network (of computers); chain (of stores)
siedzenie seat
siedzenie przy korytarzu aisle seat
siedzenie przy oknie window seat
silnik engine
siłownia gym
skala scale
skała rock
skasować validate (ticket)
skipass ski pass
sklep store
sklep bezcłowy duty-free store
sklep mięsny butcher shop
sklep muzyczny music store
sklep osiedlowy convenience store
sklep papierniczy stationery store
sklep z narzędziami hardware store
sklep z zabawkami toy store
sklep ze zdrową żywnością health food store
skóra leather; skin
skręcić v turn
skrytka bagażowa luggage locker
skrzynka pocztowa mailbox [postbox BE]
krzyżowanie intersection [junction BE]
kuter wodny jet-ski

ślepy zaułek dead end
śliski slippery
słony salty
śmieci trash [rubbish BE]
śniadanie breakfast
spa spa
śpiący policjant speed bump
spotkanie appointment (business); meeting (friends)
spóźniony late
stacja benzynowa gas [petrol BE] station
stacja kolejowa train [railway BE] station
stadion stadium
stal steel
stanowisko odprawy check-in desk (airport)
Stany Zjednoczone United States
startować take off, depart
statek ship
staw pond
steward flight attendant
strój codzienny casual clothing
stolik table
straż pożarna fire station
strażak firefighter
strój suit, clothing
strój wieczorowy evening dress
strój wizytowy formal dress
strumień stream
studiować v study
suszarka do włosów hairdryer
światła traffic light
światło light
święto państwowe national holiday
świeży fresh
szewc shoe repair [cobbler BE]
szklanka glass (non-alcoholic)
szkoła school

szlak trail
szpital hospital

T

tabletka tablet
taksówka taxi
talerz plate
targ market
telefon phone
telefon komórkowy cell phone [mobile phone BE]
telefon publiczny pay phone
telefonistka operator (phone)
terminal terminal
toaleta restroom [toilet BE]
tor track [platform BE]
tor wyścigowy racetrack [racecourse BE]
torebka purse [handbag BE]
trampolina diving board
trasa route
trasa autobusowa bus route
trawa grass
turystyka piesza hiking
tutaj here
tydzień week
tylko only

U

ubezpieczenie insurance
ugryzienie bite
ulepszony improved
ulica street
ulica jednokierunkowa one-way street
uniwersytet university
unowocześniony modernized
usługa service
uwaga attention

W

w budowie under construction

w jedną stronę one-way (trip)
wagon car (train)
wagon restauracyjny dining car (train)
wakacyjny rozkład jazdy holiday schedule [timetable *BE*]
walizka suitcase
waluta obca foreign currency
warsztat samochodowy car mechanic [repair garage *BE*]
wąwóz gorge
wejście entrance; gate (at the airport)
wełna wool
wentylator fan (electric)
wesołe miasteczko amusement park
wewnętrzny extension (phone)
wiadomość news
widelec fork
więcej more
Wielka Brytania Great Britain
wieczór evening
wiedza knowledge
winda elevator [lift *BE*]
windsurfing windsurfing
wiosna spring
włączyć turn on
własność prywatna private property
woda water
wolno slowly
wolny free (place)
wolny pokój vacancy (accommodation)
wózek bagażowy luggage cart [trolley *BE*]
wpłata deposit
wschód east
wskazówka instruction
wspinaczka rock climbing
wstęp wolny admission free

wstęp wzbroniony no access
wybrzeże coast
wydarzenie event
wydrukować *v* print
wyjście exit; gate (at the airport)
wyjście bezpieczeństwa emergency exit
wyjście przeciwpożarowe fire exit
wyjście wzbronione no exit
wykręcić dial
wyłączyć turn off
wylogować się log off
wymiana exchange
wymiana walut currency exchange
wynajem samochodów car rental [hire *BE*]
wypadek accident
wypłata cash withdrawal
wyprzedaż clearance
wyprzedzać *v* pass (car)
wysiąść get off (bus, train)
wysłać send
wysokie krzesełko highchair
występ show (in front of audience)
wzbroniony forbidden
wzgórze hill

z

z napisami subtitled
zaawansowany advanced
zabawka toy
zachód west
zaczekać wait
zadzwonić call (phone)
zagraniczny international (flight); foreign (product)
zajazd guest house
zakaźny contagious, infectious
zakupy shopping

zalogować się log on
zamawiać *v* order
zamek castle (building); lock (door)
zamknięty closed (store)
zamówienie *n* order
zamrożony frozen
zamykać *v* lock
zapakować wrap
zapakować na prezent giftwrap
zaparcie constipation
zapłacony paid
zapinać fasten (seat belt)
zapominać forget
zarezerwować reserve (tickets)
zatkany blocked
zatłoczony crowded
zatoka bay
zatrzymać się stay (at a hotel); stop (not move)
zebra pedestrian crossing
zepsuty broken
zgwałcić *v* rape
zima winter
zimno *adv* cold
zimny *adj* cold
złoto gold
zły bad
znaczek stamp
znaczek pocztowy postage stamp
znaczyć mean (meaning)
znak drogowy road sign
zniżka discount
zwolnić slow down
zwrot pieniędzy refund
zwrotny returnable

ż

żelazko *n* iron

INDEX

Berlitz pocket guide

KRAKÓW

Fifth Edition 2018

Editor: Tom Fleming
Author: Richard Schofield
Head of DTP and Pre-Press: Rebeka Davies
Picture Editor: Tom Smyth
Cartography Update: Carte
Update Production: Apa Digital
Photography Credits: AWL Images 1;
Corrie Wingate/Apa Publications 4TC,
5TC, 5MC, 5M, 6L, 7R, 11, 12, 15, 16, 22,
32, 34, 37, 38, 51, 52, 55, 58, 61, 63, 65,
71, 73, 81, 82, 86, 100, 103, 104; Gregory
Wrona/Apa Publications 4MC, 4ML,
4TL, 5T, 6R, 7, 19, 20, 28, 30, 40, 42, 44,
46, 49, 67, 69, 85, 89, 99; iStock 26, 56,
79, 91; Sco 77; Shutterstock 5M, 93, 97;
zbieg2001/Fotolia 5MC, 74
Cover Picture: iStock

Distribution
UK, Ireland and Europe: Apa Publications
(UK) Ltd; sales@insightguides.com
United States and Canada: Ingram
Publisher Services; ips@ingramcontent.com
Australia and New Zealand: Woodslane;
info@woodslane.com.au
Southeast Asia: Apa Publications (SN) Pte;
singaporeoffice@insightguides.com
Worldwide: Apa Publications (UK) Ltd;
sales@insightguides.com

**Special Sales, Content Licensing
and CoPublishing**
Insight Guides can be purchased in bulk
quantities at discounted prices. We can
create special editions, personalised jackets
and corporate imprints tailored to your
needs. sales@insightguides.com;
www.insightguides.biz